My Mothers Diary

By

A.R. Dash

This book is a work of fiction. All names and all characters; all places, events and incidents, are products of the authors imagination. Any resemblance to actual events or people, living or dead are entirely coincidental.

The author would like to take a moment for acknowledgement.

To the many people who play a part in my life, I would just like to say thank you for your continuous love you give to me although I constantly fell short. I will never be able to repay you. All I could do is promise you my undying loyal love in return. You are very much so appreciated.

On another note:

This writing journey has been a long and lonely one. I've had to be my greatest fan, my worst critic, my own inspiration as well as my own support system.

With that said,

Let the journey continue...

And to my two sons Zshquan and Arjon. This is for you guys. I love you two so much...

Published by

ARMEIN PURCELL

copyright ©2014 by Armein purcell. All rights reserved

Prologue

R.J. came home from work early with the intention of treating his pregnant wife Valarie to a night out on the town. He planned on taking her to a restaurant, afterwards, a movie. In both cases she could choose what she wanted to do.

It was the least he could do considering the fact that she had only been out of the house three times in the last month. Valarie was approaching the ninth month of a high risk pregnancy and the baby was due any day. The unborn child's safe arrival was at the top of R.J.s priority list and he would never do anything to jeopardize that but his heart ached when he thought about his wife being caged up in the house all alone while he was at work. Today was going to be different. Today, he planned on painting the town with Valarie. But when he made it home, R.J. quickly found out that he was the one in for a surprise…

R.J. stood paralyzed outside of the front door to him and his wife's home. He'd just heard his wife speak. Then he heard the words of a deep voiced man. Rage filled his body.

Jealous thoughts filled his head and disbelief crushed his heart. He wanted this moment to be part of a bad dream, but it wasn't. This was really happening.

R.J. put his ear to the door. The man's voice sounded vaguely familiar. 'What is going on?' he thought to himself. Never had R.J. allowed another man, besides himself, to step foot across the threshold of their home. To his knowledge neither had Valarie. He felt violated. The rage inside of him began to grow. His heart started to kick at his chest and he had to stop himself from kicking the door off of its hinges. R.J. was a large and powerful man. It would be easy for him to do harm to whoever it was inside of his home. He had a quick vision of himself bringing harm to both Valarie and whoever it was inside of the house. He forced himself to have hope.

Maybe there was a good reason for Valarie to be entertaining a strange man in their home. But the fact that this was taking place while R.J. was supposed to be at work pushed all rational thinking out of his head. R.J. thought about the gun stashed away on the shelf in his bedroom closet. Something bad was about to happen and R.J. felt it. Someone was about to get hurt.

R.J. took a deep breath then shoved his hand into the front pocket of his blue work uniform to retrieve his house keys. The deep voiced man said something that caused Valarie to erupt with laughter. R.J.s heart stung with pain.

His wife was the love of his life. This wasn't supposed to happen. Valarie was nine months pregnant and they were supposed to start a family and live happily ever after. R.J.

wondered what had changed between him and his wife. How long had she been involved with this love affair? Was it her secret lovers' child that she carried? R.J. was bitter with hate. He cursed Valarie's name and reputation for being so conniving and from this day forward, no matter what happened, he would look at her as the worthless whore that she was.

R.J. let out a breath of anger, and then he eased the key into the lock. His mind raced. All he had ever given her was loyalty and love. He had never even raised his voice at her. Not even once. And they'd been together for three years. He could not believe that the woman he loved was trifling. She was disrespecting him, herself, their home and worst of all the unborn child she was carrying. A vision of Valarie making love to someone else on top of a bed that R.J. brought caused R.J.s heart to pump. R.J.s last thought was that maybe he should just turn around and walk away. But he couldn't. The beast with in him, that he'd buried away so long ago was about to resurface. R.J. turned the key and burst into the apartment.

R.J. locked eyes with the deep voiced man. The stranger was shocked but he was swift. He jumped up from the couch and was on his feet in a split second. Valarie let out a gasp of surprise. R.J. never turned his head to look at her but in his peripheral vision he saw her grab at her pregnant belly.

R.J. was about to charge at the man but after taking two steps into the man's direction, he froze in astonishment. He couldn't believe who he was seeing. After what had happened between them, how could the man have the nerve to show his face, much less step foot within the walls of R.J.s home?

It was like seeing a ghost. R.J. hadn't seen this man in almost fifteen years. They just stood there staring at each other. It was as if R.J. was staring into an aging mirror. The man looked just like R.J. only years older. They were both tall but R.J. stood broad shouldered and the man's erect frame had considerable slimmed down. Both of them had neat haircuts and both of their goatees were trimmed as if they shared the same barber. The only difference was that R.J.s hair and goatee was a solid black and the man's hair was sprinkled salt and pepper. R.J. had smooth skin and the man's aging face showed signs of wrinkles. The two could have passed for twins if the man had some years erased from his life. They even shared the same style of dress. Had R.J. not been coming home from work at the car plant, where he was supervisor over all mechanics, he would not have on the grease stained blue work outfit. R.J.s typical dress code was exactly the same dress style like that of the man standing in his living room.

The man had on a plain clean pressed white button down shirt. It was neatly tucked into a pair of black slacks that was held up by a thin leather black belt. On the man's feet was a pair of plain black leather loafers. R.J. and the man had more in common than R.J. would ever admit too. They even shared the same name. R.J. was Randy junior, and the man standing in his living room, was Randy senior.

R.J. could not believe that after fifteen years of avoiding all types of communication, he now stood face to face with the man who had given him life. The whole world came to a complete stop and inside of R.J.s heart, the stabbing pain of his past life tore open like the scab of a healing wound.

CHAPTER 1.

The awkward stare of silence between father and son might have lasted forever had Valarie not stepped in. Her hand was still on her swollen belly and she still looked a bit surprised from her husband's sudden burst into the apartment.

She wobbled over to R.J.

"I didn't know who you were, charging in here like that. You almost scared this baby out of me."

R.J. heard his wife speaking but he was still somewhat lost in his daze. Valarie took hold of one of his hands then climbed to her tippy toes and placed a warm kiss on his cheek.

"Is everything okay baby?"

When he didn't respond she started rubbing his arm up and down to relieve some of his obvious tension.

"I tried calling the plant to let you know that your father and your sister had stopped by but they told me that you had already gone home for the day. It's not like you to be leaving work early. Are you feeling well baby?"

At the mention of his sister, R.J. felt another sting of pain in his chest. He had not completely given her forgiveness neither for the role she played in the dramatic pain of his past.

He pushed the unwanted feelings aside and responded to his wife.

"Yes honey, I'm okay. How are you?"

He bent down and rubbed her big belly before kissing it.

"And how's the baby?"

"He's okay."

R.J. came up and tried to place his arm around Valarie's shoulder but she pushed his arm and backed away.

"No you don't mister. You've been working on those cars all day and you have grease all over you. Don't you go touching on me until you visit the shower?"

The couple started laughing and R.J.s father joined in. R.J. cut Randy senior a slightly cold eye that Valarie didn't see and he turned his attention back to her before she did.

"You are right. And I will take a shower before I touch my queen."

Valarie blushed. R.J. continued.

"But anyway. The reason I left work early was because you have been on my mind all day and the thought of you being trapped up in this house for the last couple of weeks has been bothering my conscious. So I decided to clock out early so that I could tear the town up with my beautiful wife."

Valarie blushed harder and her eyes watered up with joy.

"Aww baby… that's so sweet of you. Come here my king. I don't care about you being all greasy no more. Give me a hug."

She threw her arms around him and when he felt her round belly press against him, all the love he had for her came to life inside of him. He wrapped his arms around her and he remembered that she was the only woman that he had ever loved besides his deceased mother. R.J. looked up at the life size portrait of his mother that hung on his living room wall and felt a bit of guilt. He hid his embarrassment by tucking his face into the cuff of his wife's neck. The fresh scent of Valarie's familiar body fragrance took hold of R.J. 'I love this girl with all of my heart' he told himself. 'How could I have ever doubted our love and been so insecure? How could I have had all of those ugly thoughts about her being with another man'? He mentally punished himself for thinking that his queen was cruel enough to disrespect herself, her king, their castle or their coming prince.

R.J. and Valarie were so caught up in their love embrace that they both seemed to have forgotten that Randy was in their home. R.J. lifted his face from the tuck of Valarie's neck and released the embrace he had on her. She released him and R.J. took a step towards his father.

Randy was looking at his son and his sons wife with soft hearted eyes. But when Randy spoke, R.J. could only describe Randy's words as deadly venom spit from a cunning snake. As R.J. got close to him, Randy looked away from his son and up at the large picture of his ex-wife. Then he looked back at R.J.

"You two remind me of your mother and I."

A jolt of electric anger shot through R.J. He cliched his teeth together tightly. It felt like his father had just spit in his face. But R.J. showed no signs of anger. He managed to conceal his true feelings in the same way he had been concealing them for over fifteen years. It was hard. And the fact that Randy had literally left R.J.s mother for dead made it harder to hide what he really felt. But he had to.

R.J. knew that he had to keep a cool head because Valarie knew nothing about his dark family secrets. He portrayed himself to her the image that he was a perfect gentlemen. And that's how she viewed him their entire three year relationship. She knew nothing about the anger that dwelled within him.

Now, because of his father's sudden presence, what he had buried away deep down inside of him so long ago threatened to explode. And if that happened, Valarie would have questions. A lot of questions.

R.J. stood there filled with guilt. Valarie had shared everything in her past with him. Even the emotional and physical abuse she suffered at the hands of her violent uncle Cory. Yet and still, the answers to the questions of R.J.s past, he planned on taking to the grave with him.

R.J. had unwanted feelings as he stood there wearing a fake smile and looking at the man who had given him life. He wished that it was Randy who was dead and not his mother.

R.J. extended a hand out to his father. He hadn't seen the man in close to fifteen years, and with that thought, there was no way he could see himself calling the man daddy. Their hands met.

"How are you Randy? This is a surprise. What brings you around?"

Randy avoided the question.

"It's good to see you R.J."

He gripped R.J.s hand powerfully. R.J. wasn't sure if this was a challenge of his man hood or not. But if it was, R.J. wasn't about to back down.

R.J. squeezed Randy's hand with just a tad bit more strength than Randy squeezed his. The whole time they looked deep into each other's eyes. Randy loosened his grip and R.J. let go of his hand. It was a small victory, never the less, it made R.J. feel good. R.J. was at the moment a king in his castle and he had just protected his kingdom. Randy was nothing more than a peasant visitor. R.J. hoped Randy understood that.

Valarie was silent but the whole time she stood there watching the two of them with a close eye.

R.J. repeated his question.

"So what brings you this way?"

Randy took a deep breath.

"Well I-I-"

He couldn't seem to finish his sentence. He looked away from his son. He dropped his eyes to the floor. Randy took another deep breath and with his eyes still avoiding his sons, he began to rub his palms together like his hands had suddenly begun to sweat.

R.J. could sense that Randy was not in his home on a social visit. Something was wrong but R.J. didn't know what. He hoped that Randy hadn't stopped by to tell him that he was ill of some sort or worst; that he was dying. To R.J. that would be more good news than bad.

R.J. looked to Valarie as if she might already know what was going on, but she just shrugged her shoulders as an indication that, she too, had no idea why Randy was acting so strange.

R.J. was again about to ask Randy what was going on but his sister Rachel came walking out of the bathroom. She was carrying some kind of book and her eyes were bloodshot red. It was obvious that she had been crying. Valarie and R.J. looked at each other in confusion. R.J. looked back to his sister then to Randy. Randy looked detached from himself. The mood in the room had gone somber.

Rachel tried to pretend that nothing was wrong. She walked over to R.J. and gave him a semi-long hug. She embraced her brother like she didn't want to let him go. Her voice was weak.

"How are you doing R.J.? I know it's been a while but it's good to see you."

R.J. marinated in the warmth of his sisters' hug.

"It's been more than a while. But I'm doing ok."

When she took her arms from around him, he took a step back and looked her up and down from head to toe. She was a spitting image of their mother, the same way he was a spitting image of their father. The resemblance between Rachel and their mother was the only reason R.J had forgiven Rachel for not being there when R.J. and their mother needed her most.

"What's wrong Rachel? Why do you look like you were crying?"

Her sad eyes quickly ran from R.J. and landed on their father before they fell to the floor. R.J. followed her gaze until his eyes too had found Randy's face. Randy looked as sad, if not sadder than Rachel. The look on Randy's face confirmed to R.J. that Randy was fully aware of what she was feeling. It was also clear that Randy shared in her pain. R.J. figured that no matter what it was that was going on, there was no doubt, Randy had something to do with it. R.J.s dislike for the man began to move around inside of him.

R.J. wanted to know what was going on. He stood there staring at Randy with a growing fire in his eyes. Valarie must've sensed that something was going on inside of R.J... She didn't say anything but she came and stood by his side.

R.J. looked away from his father back to his sister.

"Rachel, what's going on?"

She looked into her brother's face with glassy eyes. The deep wells that held her tears threatened to overflow with her next blink.

Then without warning, she broke down.

"I'm sorry R.J."

A river of tears started to pour down her face.

"I'm so sorry R.J., I swear if I could turn back the hands of time I would go back and be there for you and mommy."

At the mention of his mother, R.J.s heart skipped a beat. Valarie reached out and took hold of R.J.s hand. She held on to him as if she was frightened by the whole scene. R.J. pulled away from his wife and walked over to his sister. He placed both of his hands at the sides of her arms with a firm grip. His eyes looked carefully into her face. She looked so much like their mother. As much as he wanted to ignore the resemblance to his mother, he couldn't. But he did.

He gave her body a small shake and his voice was serious.

"What is it Rachel? What happened? What's going on?"

Rachel tears continued to flow. She looked up at him like she felt pity of some sort. She let a few more tears fall before she spoke.

"I'm alright. I'm alright R.J."

She slid out of the hold that he had on her and she turned her back to him like she was ashamed of herself. She lifted the bottom of her hands to her face and tried to wipe away the tears from her eyes. She sniffled then exhaled a gust of bottled up guilt.

She turned back around to face her brother.

"You really need to have a talk with daddy."

Rachel walked away from him without saying anything else. She stopped walking when she got in front of their father. R.J. didn't know what to think so he just stood there and watched them closely.

Rachel took the book that she was holding and handed it to Randy.

"I can't read any more of this."

He accepted the book from her then he nodded his head softly as if to imply that he understood what she was feeling. Randy reached his arms out in an attempt to comfort his daughter but she rejected him.

"No, don't do that. I'm okay."

She walked back over to R.J.

R.J. saw that more tears were forming in her eyes. She looked like she wanted to say something but couldn't find the correct words. The tears fell.

"I have to be going."

She tried to push pass R.J. and he tried to stop her.

"Rachel what is-"

She cut off his words and screamed.

"Just talk to your father!"

Rachel shoved pass R.J. and ran out of the apartment leaving the door wide open behind her. R.J. looked like he was about to go after her but pregnant Valarie, who had been standing mute the entire time, somehow beat him to the door.

"You stay here and talk to your father; I'll go after her and make sure she's okay."

Before he could say anything, Valarie was out of the apartment with the door closed behind her.

R.J. slammed his eyes into Randy!

Whatever it was that had Rachel in tears had a lot to do with his father's sudden appearance. Randy stood there rocking back and forth from one foot to the other while holding the book that Rachel had handed to him.

R.J. watched his every move and his patience was wearing thin but he held his tongue. His sisters voice echoed in his head 'just talk to your father'. It took every ounce of R.J.s discipline to remain calm.

The tone of his voice was a low and dangerous whisper.

"What is going on Randy?"

Randy was still standing near the couch he had jumped up from. He pointed to the middle cushion.

"Come and have a seat son."

R.J.s face frowned up. He was offended, and rightfully so. Randy was a guest in his home, not the other way around.

"Just say whatever it is you have to say. And my name is R.J. not son."

For a few seconds Randy stood silent. He looked like he was having trouble gathering his thoughts. Once he gathered the courage he needed, he extended his arm and held the book out to R.J.

"I've had this in my possession for some years. Actually, I've had it since your mother passed away fifteen years ago."

The mention of his mother only confused R.J. more. He wondered what her passing had to do with anything. Randy stood there holding the book out in his sons' direction.

R.J. looked down and for the first time he paid attention to the book. It looked old. So old that the black color of the book had faded so much that the book now looked gray. The book looked very familiar. It had something on the cover but from where R.J. stood he couldn't make out what it was. Suddenly, for a reason unknown to him, R.J. felt a creepy feeling crawl down his spine. He racked his brain but couldn't place where he had seen the book before. It just looked so familiar. With his eyes focused on the book, R.J. stepped closer to his father.

The thing on the cover of the book came into view just before R.J. reached out and grabbed the book from Randy's hand. On the cover was a picture of a diamond. Underneath the diamond were the words '*CRYSTAL DIAMOND DIARY*' R.J.s heart paused and he felt blood rush to his head. When the book touched his hand his legs got weak and he almost passed out. Slowly, he sat down in the seat that Randy had offered him a few minutes earlier. '*The book*' he thought to himself. The book was a book that he saw his mother writing in many times. It was the same book that taught him and his mother so much about each other. He opened the cover and underneath a caption his mother had signed her name in cursive letters. *Shirley Ann Madison.* Then it dawned on R.J. that the book had suddenly disappeared after his mother died.

R.J. was honestly puzzled. He hadn't seen the book in so long. A bunch of what's, whys and how's bounced around in his head. It felt like he was all of a sudden reconnected to something that he'd lost and forgotten. He stared down at the book in a lost haunted daze. '*What was Randy doing with this book?*'

In a dangerously slow motion he lifted his eyes. When they reached Randy's face R.J. could see that Randy must've expected for him to feel some kind of way because he didn't say anything. He just stood there looking guilty.

R.J. locked his jaws and his words crashed through clinched teeth. His breathing was barely controllable.

"Where did you get this?"

"That's what I'm here to talk to you about."

"I don't care about what you came to talk about. Where did you get this book?"

R.J. slowly rose to his feet. His six foot frame was already muscular and the built up angry air inside of him made him look large and intimidating. Randy was also tall and the matter in which R.J. stood up made Randy stop rocking back and forth. He planted his feet like he was ready to stand his ground. He looked alert and although his son was larger than him, he showed no signs of fear. But at the same time he looked overwhelmed with guilt.

Randy looked directly at his son and didn't blink.

"Like I was trying to tell you before you interrupted me, I've had the book in my possession for a long time. It's something that my wife left behind."

"Your wife?"

His words cut R.J.s chest like a sword. They were an insult to the memory of his mother. R.J. had a vision of himself charging across the room and diving into Randy's chest. The wells of R.J.s eyes became wet and he had to blink away the tears of blood that were about to fall.

"I'm not going to stand here and allow you to disrespect my mother's good name like that. You know as well as I do that you didn't treat her like a wife. She had no husband. She had no daughter, no mother or any other family. All she had was me." R.J.s eyes grew dark. "And all I had was her."

R.J. meant what he said. His words were still low but they were very aggressive and a direct warning for Randy to choose his words very carefully.

"I advise you not to speak of my mother again. Just tell me where you got this book. Then you can leave my home and never come back."

"What? You advise me to do what? Who do you think you are to tell me what I can and what I cannot say about my wife? Are you forgetting that I am Randy senior and you are Randy junior? I'm the father, not you."

Randy took two steps in R.J.s direction then he planted his feet

"Shouldn't you be the one showing a little respect here for the man who gave you life? O' yeah. By the way, she was my wife long before she was your mother."

There was a scary silence. They just stared. He wanted to make Randy eat those words. R.J. stood there trapped in a feeling that he buried away far down in the deepest part of his soul, back when he was thirteen. The thought was of him violently attacking everyone who turned their backs on him and his mother. But he couldn't attack Randy. If he did, Valarie would find out things that he didn't want her to know. He couldn't let that happen.

R.J.s blood heated to a boil. He wanted to put Randy out of his house but first he had to find out how his mother's diary ended up in Randy's hands. R.J. was able to somehow control his feelings. He stood there with hopes that Randy didn't say anything else to push his buttons. If Randy did, R.J.was going to use force to put him out of his house.

Randy's demeanor was that of a man who had gained the upper hand in a controversial situation. But his voice was not as confident as his attitude. There was weakness and sadness behind his words.

"R.J., I am your father. I've made many mistakes. And I admit that I wasn't there when you needed me most. But I'm here now."

He looked at R.J. like he was about to make a confession.

"Your mother and I went through a lot. We had some hard times. That was our business R.J. and no one else's. I'm sorry if I sound harsh but that's just the truth of the matter. I know I could've been a better man and a better father but I wasn't. I cannot change who I was or what I did in the past. Again I apologize. I beg your forgiveness R.J. and if you allowed me to, I would love a chance to be in your life."

R.J.s mouth dropped open. And for a millisecond, the forgotten little boy inside of him resurfaced and reminded him of those long days and nights when he yearned for nobody in the world but Randy. But those days were long gone and R.J. was no longer that little boy in need of a father. Randy was wasting his time.

R.J. wanted to shout a million different unpleasant words but he controlled his tongue as best he could.

"Save your breath Randy, I needed you when I was twelve and thirteen. I'm twenty-eight now. Randy I haven't needed you for a long time. Truthfully, for the last fifteen years you haven't existed to me. And even though I'm looking right at you, you still don't exist to me."

R.J. held his mother's diary in the air.

"Tell your sob story to someone who cares. All I need is for you to tell me how you ended up with this book. Then you can leave and I can continue on with my life."

"Just give me a chance to be in your life."

"Where did you get this book?"

"Son please."

R.J. screamed at the top of his lungs.

"How did you get this book?"

"I stole it okay! I stole it the day before she died. Remember that day when you let me in the house. That day I went into her room and while I was talking to her, she closed her eyes for a second and I stole it from her."

Randy stood there staring at his son with regret in his eyes. R.J. exploded. All he saw was black. Everything that he had bottled up inside of him burst at the same time. His mother's diary ended up on the floor. He charged at Randy like and out of control football player.

"Ahhh!"

Randy's eyes opened as wide as they could and he tried to back out of the way. But it was of no use. R.J. was on him like white on rice. He dropped his shoulder and crashed all two hundred pounds of his solid body into Randy's mid-section. The impact caused Randy to let out a grunt. The wind was knocked out of him instantly. They tumbled to the floor with R.J. landing on top. R.J.s hands found their way around his father's throat. He squeezed with the strength of a angry bear.

R.J. was a man possessed. He choked Randy for all the pain he had ever felt in his life. He'd been holding the anger in for way too long. Randy's eyes were watering and he tried to put up a fight but R.J. was too strong.

R.J.s voice echoed throughout the room.

"I HATE YOU!!!"

Randy tried to beg for mercy but only the sounds of choked up gags made it out of his mouth. The sound of Randy's cries only made it worst.

R.J. continued his attack.

"I HATE YOU!!! I HATE YOU!!! I HATE YOU!!!"

Randy looked like he was about to lose consciousness but R.J. didn't care. He looked down at his father and all he saw was his enemy. R.J. cocked his head back and viciously slammed his forehead into the bridge of Randy's nose. A bone cracked and blood splattered.

"Ughh!"

Was the last sound from Randy before he gave up fighting.

But R.J. wasn't done with his assault.

He raised one of his powerful hands far above his head and formed a mighty fist. Just before he smashed it against Randy's bloody face, he felt someone grab him by the wrist of his raised arm.

R.J. snatched his arm away from whoever it was and jumped up off of his father ready to attack whoever it was trying to save Randy. In a swift motion he turned around and raised his fist. He had become a madman.

"AHHH!!!"

R.J. stood in his living room in attack mode. And just before he swung a mighty blow he saw that it was Valarie. She jumped back and ducked her head down in between her arms. She looked beyond petrified. Tears of fear dropped from her eyes and she sounded like a scared child begging not to be abused.

"Please don't hit me Cory! Please don't hit me! I won't do it again!"

She was calling R.J. by the name of her abusive uncle. Her breathing was in short pants.

"Please don't hit me Cory! Please don't hit me again!"

The sight of his petrified wife quickly sobered him up from his drunken rampage. He lowered his hand and snatched his wife into his arms. He had done something terrible and Valarie had witnessed it.

R.J. squeezed his wife against his chest.

"I'm sorry Valarie. I'm sorry. I'm sorry. I don't remember what happened."

She continued to breathe in spurts and pout against his chest. R.J. held Valarie against his body and looked down at Randy. Randy's hands were covering his face and he moved his head from one side to the other as he let out cries of pain. When he removed his hands from his face R.J. saw that he was a bloody mess but didn't care. He hoped that Randy's nose looked broken.

R.J. rocked his wife back and forth in the love and safety of his arms as he stared down at Randy with hate and venom in his heart. R.J. knew one thing. Had Valarie not come in when she did, more than likely, he would have killed his father.

CHAPTER

2.

 The emergency room waiting area was spotless and the floor had a mop and glow shine. It felt like the air conditioner was on full blast and R.J.s burning rage had calmed down considerably. Valarie, R.J. and about five other people were scattered around the room. Each person looked lost in their own individual troubles.

 Valarie and R.J. sat next to each other in silence. They hadn't said two words to each other ever since she'd begged him to bring his father to the hospital.

 R.J. looked at his wrist and his watch showed that forty five minutes had crawled by since he had taken the seat next to his wife. R.J. really didn't want to be there waiting on his so called father. He remembered his attack on Randy and felt no remorse. He thought that when he agreed to bring the man to get medical attention it meant that he was going to drop him off at the door and be done with it. But when Randy got out of the car, Valarie also got out of the car and she led him into the emergency room. R.J. just sat there watching as his wife guided his bloody victim through the automatic doors. Randy's shirt was so drenched in blood that it no longer looked white. And with his blood stained hands covering his nose and mouth he wasn't able to make it through the emergency room doors without attracting the attention he needed to obtain help. A nurse came running and quickly she ushered Randy into the direction of the help that he so desperately needed. R.J. watched the whole scene without a care in the world but after ten minutes had passed and Valarie still hadn't returned to the car, R.J. decided to join her in the waiting area.

R.J. was ready to go home. He would not lose any sleep over the incident with Randy and he had high hopes of never crossing paths with the thief again. R.J. sat there aggravated and wondered just how far Valarie was going to go to extend a helping hand to someone that he hated. He was tempted to get up and leave both of them right there where they were at but he knew that if he did that then the chances of him getting back in good with Valarie would be minimal.

R.J. stood up and looked down at his pregnant wife. She sat there staring blankly at the wall in front of her.

"Valarie, are you ready to leave?"

She looked up at R.J. with eyes that looked like they would rather be looking at anything but him.

"No I'm not ready to go. I know that I don't know your father well but I refuse to leave him alone in such terrible condition."

She turned her attention back to the wall.

R.J. wanted to dispute his wife's decision but he knew her well enough to know that it didn't matter if he kicked, scratched, cried or held his breath to his face turned blue, she was not going to move. She was going to sit in that same emergency room seat until the doctors were done fixing on Randy.

He wished that she didn't care but she did. He was about to say something else but he bit his tongue and swallowed some words that she would just have ignored anyway. He bluff like he was going to leave but it didn't work so he politely sat back down next to his wife and joined her in silence. He couldn't believe that she was siding with the enemy. He wondered what she'd have to say if he told her what Randy had done. How Randy had stolen something from his mother on the day before she passed away. The thoughts only made R.J.s temperature rise so he pushed the thoughts from his mind.

For the next twenty-five minutes or so, the channels of R.J.s mind flipped back and forth between the happiness he felt for now having possession of his mother's priceless diary and the worry that clouded him for not knowing what he was going to tell Valarie when her nerves finally settled down and she began asking her questions. He sat there trying to clear his mind, there was no use in racking his brain for answers that he didn't have. He would just have to handle those problems when they surfaced. But one thing was certain; he could not let Valarie find out about the ghost of his past. He had to keep all of his skeletons in the closet and take them with him to his grave.

    R.J. leaned back in the emergency room chair that he was sitting in and closed his eyes and tried to relax. Then, without warning, a sudden vision of his mother lying helplessly in pain on her death bed flooded every inch of space in his mind. There was never room for another thought in his head when these images appeared. R.J. sat there and silently panicked. Valarie didn't notice, but her husband sat next to her in a state of shock. He was frozen with fear because he knew that he was about to relive the same nightmare that tormented him for an entire year after his mother died. Back then, he was nothing but a helpless twelve year old little boy who was frightened beyond his years. As he was about to find out, age was nothing but a number because although he was now a grown man, he still felt the same fear that he felt when he was a kid and the unwanted thoughts entered his mind.

    No one in the emergency room noticed, but R.J. had literally transformed back into the scared and lonely child he once was. R.J. was about to co-star in a filmed scene of pain. R.J. began to experience the saddest emotions he'd ever known.

    In his mind's eye R.J. saw his mother; her name was Shirley Ann Madison. She was lying on her back stretched out across her death bed waiting for help. Help from anyone. There is a thin line that separates temporary life from eternal death and she looked as if she couldn't hold on to the side that gave her life for too much longer.

Her eyes rained tears. She looked weaker than she had ever looked. When she noticed R.J. she raised her arm in his direction. Her face curled in agony. Using all of her tiny strength, she extended her fragile hand and reached out for help from her loving son. But R.J. was too young to know what he was supposed to do to help her. He wished that someone older was there to help his mother because all he could do was cry, feel helpless and stand there watching her as she suffered. He stood in her bedroom feeling useless. He wanted her to tell him what to do. Then her lips began to move and form words but no sound came out. All R.J. wanted to do was help her, but he couldn't. He would have done anything but was only able to watch her squirm in pain while her swollen eyes poured out rivers of tears.

His mother continued to reach for him and it seemed that the longer it took for him to help her, the more she cried. R.J. knew that all she wanted was to be helped. But no one else cared. He was the only person willing to help her but was too young to complete the task. He desperately needed her to tell him what to do. She continued to form words with her mouth but was too weak to push out the sounds. R.J. lifted his open hand then extended his arm towards his suffering mother as far as he could. His small hand wanted to touch her. But in this vision for some reason no matter how hard he tried, their hands were never able to touch. The only thing they were able to do was watch one another suffer as they both cried out fountains of agonizing tears.

Right there in the emergency room, R.J.s body began to shake. He went into more of a panic. From somewhere, he heard his name being called but he didn't know where his name was being called from. He didn't know what was happening. He was torn between two worlds. His adult life and his childhood memories.

His eyes flew open. There was someone standing directly in front of him. A lady. He stared into her face. He didn't know who she was. She reached out and began shaking him by his shoulder. He didn't respond, he just sat there staring blankly into her unknown face. She moved her lips and he heard the familiar sound of her voice calling out his name.

"R.J., R.J."

It was Valarie, his wife. Where did she come from? R.J. blinked his eyes then quickly looked away from Valarie and surveyed his surroundings. He was sitting in a waiting room of a hospital. Immediately he recalled the attack on Randy and remembered exactly what was going on. He looked back up at his wife. She stood there watching him closely as if she had a question in her head and was trying to read him for the answer.

R.J. ran his hand down his face and felt beads of sweat at the sides of his nose. He stood up from his seat as casually as possible.

"I must've fallen asleep. What happen? Are we ready to leave yet?"

Valarie's eyes searched R.J.s face. She looked like she wanted to say something but she held back her words. It was as clear as day to see that she knew something was wrong.

"What is it Valarie? What's wrong with you? Why are you looking at me like that?"

"No reason R.J... No reason at all."

She looked away from her husband into the direction of the double doors. R.J.s natural reaction caused him to look in the same direction. He saw Randy and the sight of the man caused his insides to jerk like he had just hit a speed bump.

As Randy came through the doors, his eyes zoned in and locked on his son. R.J. held Randy's gaze and took a deep breath. He noticed that Randy didn't have the arrogant look that he had earlier. A white bandage was taped across his nose and beneath both of his eyes he had black rings. He looked like a raccoon and his face sagged with sadness. Randy still had on the bloody shirt. He looked like he could've been the poster boy for what a broken man should look like. His pathetic appearance didn't move R.J. in the least bit. To R.J., the man looked the same way every thief should look after they have stolen something.

R.J. looked away from him just to find Valarie's waiting eyes still watching him like she was doing another inspection of the situation at hand. She tried to avoid R.J.s eyes and changed her demeanor as if everything was okay.

She moved closer to him and spoke low enough so that only he could hear her.

"Listen R.J., I don't have a clue as to what is going on. Nor do I have any idea why your sister ran out of the house crying. Or know what took place between you and your father when I left the apartment. And I definitely do not know why my husband is acting so strange."

She took her hand and lightly touched R.J. on the chin and turned his head in her direction before finishing.

"What I do know is that you rarely speak with your sister; from what you told me, you barely knew your father; that your mother passed away when you were young; and that there's obviously a lot more going on with you and your family then you shared with me."

R.J. felt a wave of guilt as he looked into his wife's eyes and listened.

"This is scaring me R.J… You're scaring me. But we will deal with that later. Right now you have to straighten this mess out with your father."

Valarie left her words hanging in the air then turned away and walked over to Randy who was just standing there looking lost. When she reached Randy, she said something that somehow caused him to smile, and then she led him out of the hospital to R.J.s car. For the entire ride home, Valarie and Randy made conversation and R.J. didn't say a word.

When they made it back to the apartment, Valarie guided Randy over to the couch where he had been sitting earlier. When it looked as though Randy was comfortable she looked away from him and over to R.J.

"Can you please excuse me for a moment Randy?"

Randy nodded his head and shortly after, Valarie and R.J. disappeared down the hallway to their bedroom. Once inside the bedroom, R.J. closed the door and spoke for the first time in almost an half an hour.

"Why did you bring him here? I don't want that man in my house."

"For Christ sake R.J., he's your father. Look at him why don't you. He looks like he has been in a war."

R.J.s voice flared up.

"I don't care what he looks like. I don't want him in my house!"

"Calm down and lower your voice, he can hear you."

"So what if he can hear me! I don't want him here and that's that!"

Valarie looked at him for an annoying second then left him standing there in his emotions. She walked over to the dresser and started to go through R.J.s shirt draw. R.J. knew exactly what she was doing but he felt the need to ask anyway.

"What are you doing? Why are you going through my shirt draw? I know you don't plan on giving him anything of mine."

Her neck snapped towards R.J.

"I'm getting him some decent clothes to put on. What's the matter with you? What did he do to you to have you acting like this?"

He didn't answer. Valarie reached back into the drawer and found a change of clothes for Randy.

"I'm going to get him changed into these clothes. Afterwards I would like for you to at least hear what he has to say. If not for nothing else, can you do it for me?"

She looked at him with pleading eyes.

"We all make mistakes R.J."

She walked out of the room and left him standing there with his thoughts. And all he could think about is how much he did not want to hear what Randy had to say.

R.J. walked over to the dresser and closed the drawer that she left open. He was about to go out into the living room to tell Randy how he felt about not wanting to hear what he had to say but as he turned away from the dresser he caught a glimpse of himself in the mirror. He stood there and stared at his reflection. His face sagged with an expression of worry that made him look a few years older than he was. The stress he felt had him looking more like his father than ever. R.J.

closed his eyes, dropped his chin into his chest and shook his head. Suddenly he had a thought that may solve his problems. His neck jerked back up into the mirror. *'Yes'* He thought to himself. He could hear Randy out and pretend to listen to what he had to say. If he did that, he might be able to avoid a lot of Valarie's questions. Then he had another thought. He could also hear what Randy's excuse was for being such a sorry father. R. J. had never known why Randy was never there in his life; if he took the time to listen to what Randy had to say than maybe he could close out an unfinished chapter of his past. He was sure his plan would work but first he had to take a shower and get out of his work clothes, so he grabbed some underclothes and headed for the bathroom.

After the shower, R.J. threw on a t-shirt and some jeans and headed for the living room. He could hear Valarie and Randy well off into a conversation. When he cut the corner, both his wife and his father paused their convo and looked up at him. A split second later they carried on as if he hadn't entered the room.

The first thing to catch R.J.s eye was the shirt of his that Valarie had given to Randy. It looked exactly like the one that had been covered in blood. The shirt fit Randy loosely, but had it been one or two sizes smaller, there would have been no way of telling that Randy now wore a different shirt. The similarity left R.J. with a bad taste in his mouth.

R.J. looked away and as he did so his eyes gazed pass the coffee table and he caught a glimpse of his mother's diary. He couldn't believe that he was looking at the same book that he and his mother enjoyed together almost fifteen years earlier.

R.J. moved as if he was magnetically drawn to the book. He floated across the room as if he was riding a cloud and scooped the book up into the safety of his hands. Valarie and Randy stopped talking and both of them watched closely. R.J. paid them no mind. He was completely transfixed on the book. Although the shade of the entire book was dull, the picture of the diamond still held a pretty glow. R.J. ran his fingers across the engraved picture of the diamond. He flipped open the cover and saw his mother's signed name underneath a caption that read; *100 Questions that lets you get to know someone, while getting to know yourself.* A smile plastered across R.J.s face.

He turned the page to the first question. It read; *if you could change one law, what would it be?*

Underneath the question, R.J.s mother had written in her answer but R.J. remembered what it was before he read it. He recalled her saying that she would outlaw cigarettes. He looked down and saw that what he had remembered was the exact answer that she had given. A bigger smile crossed his face.

Valarie stopped her conversation with Randy and looked at R.J. with interest. She stood up and toted her big belly over to the reclining chair where R.J. was sitting and sat on the arm. She looked down over R.J.s shoulder at the book.

"What are you reading Baby? What has you smiling like that?"

"It's my mothers diary."

Valarie shot her eyes away from the book like she was looking at something that she shouldn't have been looking at.

"Oh… I apologize; I wasn't trying to be nosy."

"No… No… it's okay."

It was obvious that Randy hadn't told Valarie about the diary.

"It's my mother's diary, but not the kind of diary that you think it is."

"What do you mean? There is only one kind of diary. Am I not correct?"

R.J. closed the book and showed her the cover. Randy sat quietly as R.J. tried to explain to Valarie what kind of diary it was.

"No baby you're not being nosy. This is not a personal diary, it's a Crystal Diamond Diary and inside of it there are one hundred questions. Really good questions I might add. And the purpose of the diary is to allow two people that care for each other the chance to really get to know one another."

"It sounds interesting."

R.J.s voice unconsciously became excited.

"That's because it is."

He opened the book to a random page.

"See, if you and I were trying to get to know each other and we had a Crystal Diamond Diary, I would ask you-"

He looked down at the open book and pointed his finger to one of the questions on the page.

"What is one place you have to visit before your life comes to an end?"

He didn't give her time to respond.

"Being that I know you so well, I don't need this book to know that you would say Paris."

Valarie sounded pleasingly surprised.

"Awww baby, I told you about wanting to go to Paris back when we first met. That was over three years ago and you still remember."

R.J. looked up at his wife with a confident smile that quickly changed when he heard the sound of Randy's deep voice.

"Your mother always wanted to visit Jamaica."

R.J. looked at Randy with sharp eyes. Then he looked down at his mothers diary to see if Randy was correct. Underneath the question, his mother had answered that she wanted to visit Jamaica. A touch of jealousy pinched R.J…

Then he remembered that Randy had stolen the diary so long ago that he probably knew the answer to every question like he knew the back of his hand.

R.J.s voice was filled with annoyance.

"Of course you know the answer to that. You've had her diary in your possession for fifteen years... I don't doubt that you know every answer to every question in this book."

Randy stared at R.J. and spoke without blinking.

"Actually I've never opened that book."

R.J. felt lied to. He looked at Randy like he was a joke.

"Do you seriously want me to believe that?"

"Yes I would like for you to believe that. Also, you can believe that I didn't need any book, and I still don't need a book to know about the lady that I loved."

For a second R.J. felt like Randy was once again being arrogant. A cluster of aggressive words filled his head. He was about to speak his mind but remembered that he had to play nice with Randy to throw Valarie off of the scent to his secret past.

He looked down at his mother's diary and flipped through a few pages.

"You claim that you knew her very well and I highly doubt it so let's just put it to the test. What was her favorite color?"

"Pink and purple."

R.J. looked down, Randy was right. R.J. went to the next question.

"What was her favorite food?"

"Calamari… Don't do this R.J."

He was right again. R.J. ignored him and turned a few pages in the diary.

"If she could have brought someone back from the dead, who would it have been?"

Randy answered the question without hesitation.

"Her grandmother."

"What is something that she thinks is normal that others might think is weird?"

"She liked to eat plain onions."

R.J.s body began to warm up with frustration. There was no way Randy knew that much about his mother without having read the diary. He was determined to prove that Randy didn't know her as well as he thought he did. R.J. grabbed a chunk of pages and turned to the middle of the diary. The page he landed on did not have any questions. Instead, in big black letters were the words '*A TIME IN MY LIFE*'. Underneath the words, his mother had again signed her name. *Shirley Ann Madison.* R.J. turned the page and in his mother's hand writing there was a long paragraph. The paragraph began with a sentence that crushed R.J.s heart.

I love randy soooo much. He has always been good to me. I'll never love another man the way I love him.

R.J. paused in shock. He did not want to believe what he'd just read so he slammed the book shut. For a few seconds he just sat there staring at the diamond on the cover of the diary. The diary had more to it then he thought. Not only did the diary ask a hundred questions, but in the back of the diary it also had a section to write in just like an ordinary diary.

R.J. raised his eyes up into Valarie's direction. She looked like she was enjoying the fact that Randy was able to answer the questions correctly.

"Valarie, this is my mother's diary."

"We know that honey. But why did you stop asking questions?"

She winked her eye at Randy and smiled. Randy smiled back. Again R.J. was pinched by jealousy.

"No Valarie you don't understand… This is her real diary."

Valarie's smile slowly faded.

"You mean her personal diary?"

R.J. nodded his head then looked down at the diary. There was a moment of silence. R.J. sat there staring at the diary and the words his mother had written replayed in his head. He didn't understand how his mother could have loved Randy so much. Randy wasn't even man enough to help her raise their children. R.J. was truly confused and out of nowhere, he had a sudden urge to find out what his mother had written in the diary.

R.J. lifted his eyes to find that Randy had never stopped looking at him. R.J. thought to himself that maybe he was being a little too hard on his father. And there was only one way to find out, and that was by reading his mother's diary. Maybe there was something in the diary that would help R.J. to understand some of the chaos that went on in his family all those years ago.

R.J. reopened his mother's diary and turned the pages until he found the section that read *'A TIME IN MY LIFE'*, and then he handed the book to his wife.

"Would you mind reading this?"

"No R.J. this is your mother's personal thoughts. I can't read this."

"I know. That's why I want you to read it. There are a lot of unanswered questions that she may be able to answer."

R.J. rose up out of the reclining chair to let his wife have the seat and he went over to the couch and sat next to Randy.

___CHAPTER___

___3.___

Valarie sat there with the open diary in her lap. She looked at both her husband and his father.

"Are you both sure you want me to read this?"

The father and son looked at each other. While looking directly into Randy's eyes, R.J. spoke to his wife.

"I don't have a problem with it."

Randy's eyes didn't flinch as he gave his answer.

"I don't have a problem. Go ahead and read it."

So Valarie began reading; she began to read the painful words of Shirley Ann Madison. The pleading words of a mother crying out from her grave.

∞∞∞∞∞∞∞∞∞∞∞∞∞∞∞∞∞∞∞∞∞∞∞∞∞∞∞∞∞∞∞

I love Randy sooo much. He's always been good to me. I will never love another man the way I love him. And I know in my heart that no other man could ever love me as much as he does… we've been together for over a decade and a half and he has never hurt me, at least not intentionally. I know he was only trying to help me and the kids, but he will never know how much pain he left me in when he wrote them two bad checks and ended up in prison. He'll never understand how much harder things got when he left. All I've ever known was Randy, and when he left, I didn't know how to be out in the world by myself; especially with the children. We needed him more than ever, and not only that, but sometimes I got so lonely that it hurt. I was so sad and all I needed was someone to talk too. Then, as if sent directly to me, a man came into my life. His name is Jody, and Jody is a really good man to me.

As I lay here in bed with my lover of the past two months, my thoughts began to wonder about Randy, my incarcerated husband. His one year prison sentence will be up in less than six weeks and I still haven't told him about Jody. Nor have I spoken to Jody about the relationship we share and what I plan to do when Randy comes home. Jody often brings up the question of whom do I plan to be with once Randy is released but I continuously avoid the topic. Or at least I was able to avoid the topic until earlier tonight. I avoid the topic because I'm really not sure of whom I plan to be with when Randy does come home. The truth of the matter is that my heart is with Randy. He's the only man that I have ever known intimately up until I slept with Jody. I've been with Randy ever since I was a little girl and we now have two beautiful children, Rachel who is thirteen and Randy Jr. who is ten. I do not want to break my family up. But I would be lying to myself and to the world if I was to say that my feelings for Jody aren't extremely strong.

When Jody came to me, he came to me as a stranger. Then we became friends. He was fun from the start. He knew exactly what to do to make me smile. If I was down, he knew exactly what to say to make me feel better. He was kind; respectful. He knew what I liked; what I didn't like. Sometimes he predicted me so accurately that it was scary. He never said or did the wrong thing; when it came to me, he almost never made mistakes. If I didn't know any better, I would've thought that prior to meeting me, Jody was taught what to do to win me over.

It was maybe two weeks after meeting Jody that he showed signs of wanting me to be his lady. I was flattered but I was also a married lady. So I did the right thing. I told him about Randy. Afterwards, I thought that he would stop coming around and stop calling me because he couldn't have me. But to my surprise, that didn't happen. Like a true friend, Jody told me that he totally understood as well as respected the loyalty and love that I had for my husband. And we remained honest friends for the next five months. (Honest friends...yeah right). Who was I fooling? The more time that passed, the more he wanted me. I was sure of this because as more time went on, deep down inside, I found myself also wanting him. Truthfully, I found myself secretly yearning for him. A few times I even dreamed about him, but I never told him. And I didn't have to. I didn't have to because Jody wasn't stupid by a long shot; Jody knew exactly what was going on. But he was smart; he exercised patience and played his cards perfectly. We didn't cross any lines and we danced around the inner feelings we had for each other for as long as we could. Eventually, the secret passion and desire for one another reached a peak that neither of us cared to control. The inevitable was bound to happen so we decided to stop fighting it. We agreed that due to my situation we could be no more than friends. And that's what we did, we remained friends, but we added benefits. We did this under two rules; the first rule was that neither one of us could bring feelings to the table; the second rule was that when Randy came home we were going to stop seeing each other without argument. That was then...

Now Jody tells me that he loves me and he doesn't let a day go by without showing me how much. The crazy thing is that although I have never said 'I love you' back to him, in my heart I know I do. Why wouldn't I?

For the past six months Jody has been my everything. When I'm soft, he's my rock. When I'm weak, he's my strength. When I'm in need, he's my support. It doesn't matter the reason, if I need him, he's there. And not only for me. He's also there for the kids, R.J. and Rachel. If their ever in need and there is something Jody can do to help, he does it without question. I don't have to ask him twice. If he has what they need, he gives it and asks for nothing in return.

I'm so confused...

Plus, with Jody I feel free. I can do as I like and come and go as I please. I don't have to answer to no one, nor am I obligated to any responsibilities. But none of that really matters. In a nutshell, I am just use to Jody.

Earlier this evening, my head was resting on his chest and as I laid there caressing the six pack of muscles in his stomach; Jody began to speak from what sounded like the core of his being.

"So what are you going to do Shirley Ann?"

I swear. With my ear pressed against his chest, it sounded as though the words were being spoken directly from the core of his heart. It kind of scared me.

I leaned up off of him and gazed down into his handsome face. His beautiful eyes were full of seriousness. They were demanding an answer. In the background, soft music played. Someone was singing there heart out about how when a man loves a woman, she could do no wrong.

Jody continued to look up at me as I stared down at him in silence. When the guilt inside of me became too much, I looked away from him and laid my head back down on his chest. His solid body felt the way a real man's body should feel.

"I don't know Jody. I really do not know what I am going to do."

For the next couple of moments the room was quiet of our voices. I listened to the sweet beating of his heart and he gently stroked my silky hair as I lightly traced his navel with my finger.

I wondered what he was thinking about.

"What do you think I should do Jody?"

When I asked the question, the pattern of his heart beat suddenly changed. He let out a hard serious sigh.

"Do you want me to lie to you or tell you the truth?"

"I think you should pack up and move away with me."

"Stop joking. This is serious."

Jody rose up to a sitting position, causing me to rise with him. When our eyes met, he looked at me with sincerity. His eyes were so soft.

"Shirley Ann. I've never been more serious in my life. I love you. I'm in love with you... I'm in love with you and I don't want to lose you."

His words gave me a warm feeling. I believed every word that he said. I found myself entertaining his thought.

"What about my children?"

"You can bring them. I love your children. I promise to be a good father to them."

"But what about Randy?"

His voice became strong.

"Forget Randy... what about me? What about you? What about us?"

Although his words were aggressive, his eyes remained soft and full of love. I had to turn my head.

"I need more time to think."

"You don't have time."

We were quiet for a second. I sat there with my legs hanging off of the bed. He came and sat as close to me as possible. His hand lightly touched my back.

"I've been saving up Shirley Ann. I have enough for us to start a new life together. We can---"

"Stop Jody... please... I need time."

"You don't have time!"

"But I need it."

He snatched away from me and got up off of the bed. I watched him. He paced the room two times in anger then he stopped directly in front of me.

"I can't wait forever. I mean, I do love you with all of my heart and I don't mean to sound harsh but I'm going to have to start worrying about me. I have to get on with my life."

His words stabbed at my chest like a sharp pain. My body tightened up and Jody must've sensed it. He sat back down next to me and reached over to embrace me but I pulled away from him and moved to the far corner edge of his queen size bed and sat there with my back to him. I felt bitter and unwanted.

"Oh... I see... You have to get on with your life... yeah Jody, just like that? Forget about me right?"

I knew that I sounded like a selfish child but his words hurt me. On the inside, one part of me was saying that I should use his words against him as a way to end our relationship and maybe that's what I should have done, but I didn't. I couldn't. Because another part of me wanted to pick up and leave with him and never come back.

I'm so confused...

He called my name out and brought me out of my thoughts.

"Shirley Ann... Did you hear me say anything about me forgetting you?"

I thought his words were strong with attitude. I didn't respond to what he'd said. He moved closer to me but he didn't touch me.

"Now is not the time to be acting like a baby. You got yourself into this mess; now make a decision to get yourself out."

His words shocked me. He'd never been so blunt. My head twisted in his direction. His face was hard. It showed no pity. We stared at each other. A lump formed in my throat, and I exploded.

"It's not that easy Jody!"

"Yes it is!"

My tears were many.

"No it's not that easy and you know it's not!"

"Yes it is! And don't tell me what I know! Just make a decision and tell me what it is!"

"I can't!"

"You can!"

"No I can't!"

"Why can't you?"

"I just can't!"

"Why!"

"Because!"

"Because what?"

"Because I love you ok!!! Because I love you!!!"

It was the first time I had ever said the words to him. For a quick second, the world stop spinning. I sat on the bed looking up at him with a face soaked in tears. He stood there looking down at me in a stunned daze. Then he rushed at me.

"Shirley Ann... Baby."

He took me into his strong arms and held me tenderly. For a few minutes I cried like a baby against his chest. Then he kissed me on the top of my head and whispered,

"I love you too."

I cried harder. He held me tighter.

When I found the strength to look up into Jody's face, I was surprised to see that he too had tears in his eyes. It was the first time me and a man cried together. Then Jody kissed me. And we made love like we were never going to see each other again...

∞∞∞∞∞∞∞∞∞∞∞∞∞∞∞∞∞∞∞∞∞∞∞∞∞∞∞∞∞∞∞

Valarie stopped reading the diary... She slowly closed it and looked at R.J. with caution. R.J. was sitting there with his eyes closed. He was imagining his mother going through her romantic dilemma. Almost all of R.J.s memories of his mother were memories of pain, but for the first time he was able to visualize her as the center of attention and affection. It was the softest thought he'd ever had about her and a total contradiction of how she suffered in her last days: when it seemed no one cared enough to even visit her as she lay in need on her death bed. R.J. wondered who Jody was.

A few moments of dead silence passed before R.J. realized that Valarie had stopped reading. He came out of his daydream and his eyes popped open. He looked at his wife and was happy that his mother's words hadn't exposed his family's dysfunctional history.

"Why did you stop reading?"

"Because at the bottom of the page there is a single rose that she must've drawn to end this section. But its many more pages to the diary."

She held the book up so that R.J. could see the rose that his mother had drawn. R.J. smiled. He thought it was a pretty drawing.

Valarie turned her attention to Randy. He was hunched over with his elbows on his knees and his head on his forearms. R.J. also looked towards him. He had forgotten that his father was there. Randy kept his head down. R.J. was touched to find out that Randy had sacrificed his freedom to put food on the table for his family. R.J. thought that maybe he had been a little bit hard on him. Then he thought about what Valarie had just read and suddenly felt pity for his father. To hear the words of his deceased wife feelings for another man had to hurt. R.J. couldn't imagine if the shoe was on the other foot and Valarie was the one who felt that way about another man.

R.J. slid over and placed a hand on his father's back.

"Are you okay Randy?"

Randy slowly lifted his head up from his arms. He looked crushed. He inhaled deeply, then released the breath from his lungs.

"Yeah, I'm okay."

But R.J. could tell that he wasn't. Randy looked at the diary and continued speaking.

"Hearing this is like re-living a nightmare."

R.J. took what Randy said and tried to twist the words so that he could get Randy to confess that he had previously read the diary. He looked at Randy with accusing eyes.

"I thought you said that you never open the book."

"No… No… No… I have never opened the book. I swear. What I mean is that I lived through what your mother is talking about. It's my fault all of that stuff happened."

Valarie tried to console Randy.

"It's not your fault Randy; you were incarcerated when all of that took place. There was nothing you could do."

"Not exactly… I mean, I was incarcerated but so was Jody. He was my cellmate for the first six months that I was in jail."

Randy looked his son deep in the eyes."

"And for the entire six months that we were cellmates, I told him everything there was to know about Shirley Ann. All I did everyday was talk about her, you and your sister. You guys were my pride and joy. I told Jody everything about you. Everything about your mother. Her likes. Her dislikes. And everything else I could think of. I didn't mean too, but I missed her so much that all I could think of to talk about was her. I even talked to him about our love life. Jody use to listen with undivided attention and at the end of each conversation he would always say that he was going home to get the same kind of love that me and your mother had. How was I suppose to know that the creep was talking about finding my wife? And to make matters worse, when he left, that dirt bag stole a picture of your mother along with an envelope containing her address. Then he did exactly what he said he was going to do. He found the love that I had and made it his own. I was so stupid."

Valarie and R.J. both sat there with stunned looks on their faces. R.J. was at a complete loss of words. The understanding he'd never had for his father begin to grow at a rapid pace. A strong urge to hug and comfort the man who had given him life tempted R.J. but his manly pride wouldn't allow him to do so.

Valarie once again was the one to break the awkward silence.

"Wow Randy that was really messed up. I'm sorry that happened to you but you shouldn't blame yourself. Jody is the one at fault. He was wrong for what he did to you."

"Thank you Valarie, but I am the one to blame. I believe in my heart that I was wrong. I should've kept my personal business to myself."

R.J. was surprised to find himself joining Valarie in her effort to ease Randy's pain.

"All you did was trust him Randy. You weren't wrong. You were in a vulnerable state and Jody took advantage of your weakness."

R.J. had a new person to direct his anger towards. Jody. A man that he never even met. A man who stole his mother's heart away from his father. And also the man who unknowingly robbed him of the chance to have a father.

"Jody was a loser!!!"

Both Randy and Valarie looked stunned by R.J.s sudden outburst, but neither one of them said a word. They just watched as he vented with the anger of a steaming loco motive.

"You confessed the undying love you had for your family to him because you thought he was a friend and what did he do? I'll tell you what he did! He took your family away from you! He was less than a man for that and I hate him!!!"

Valarie tried to rush over to her husband's side but because of her pregnant belly, she wasn't as quick as Randy was to get up out of his seat. Randy stopped at R.J.s side. He looked like he wanted to embrace his son but wasn't sure if he should so he stood as close to him as possible without feeling like he was invading his space.

"It's okay R.J. you don't have to be upset. What's done is done. We can't change the past, but we can work on the future."

R.J. looked up at his father and felt guilty for the way he had treated him.

"Your right Randy and I apologize for what happened earlier."

Randy looked surprised.

"It's okay, I completely understand."

Valarie observed the father and son pair with a smile on her face. Randy turned his head away from R.J. towards Valarie.

"Now if you don't mind, I'm really eager to hear what else is in that diary."

Valarie looked at R.J. and he just nodded his head as an indication that he agreed with his father.

"So am I Randy… So am I."

They sat down at the same time and waited for Valarie to begin.

A humbling silence fell over the room as Valarie re-opened the diary.

CHAPTER 4.

I can't believe that R.J. pulled a crazy stunt like that. I love my ten year old son to death but the only way I will forgive him is if God himself gives me the strength.

Last night was a night that I will never forget. At around nine o'clock, I tucked R.J. into bed, as I do every night. Later on, when I went to check on him I found that he wasn't in his bed. I thought it was very odd. Then I noticed that his bedroom window was open. Automatically, I knew something was wrong. That's when I saw there was a folded up piece of paper on his bed; It turned out to be a runaway letter. I picked it up. His words were written in pencil and his message was short and simple.

'I AM NOT COMING BACK UNTIL MY FATHER IS HERE...'

Immediately I panicked, ran to the phone and dialed Jody's number. He was the only person I had to turn too, but his phone just rang out. He probably saw that it was me calling and purposely didn't answer because I still hadn't given him an answer to who I was going to be with when randy came home. I called three more times and got the same response, no answer.

I didn't have time to be mad. I had to go and find my baby. I grabbed a sweater and just before I ran out of the house, I picked up a box cutter and stuffed it into my pocket then I stormed out into the darkness of the night.

It was well after midnight. I'd been searching the neighborhood for over an hour. Still I hadn't found R.J. I walked aimlessly. About thirty stressful minutes later, I found myself drifting deeper and deeper into the unsafe parts of the city. Armed with only a box cutter and motherly love, I stole through the dark streets determined to find my child.

The night air was getting colder by the minute and the thin sweater that I wore did little to keep me warm, but I kept pushing. With my shoulders hunched and my hands holding my sweater closed across my chest I traveled through neighborhoods that were calm and empty. The houses to both the left and right of me were quiet and still. All lights were out. More than likely the houses were occupied by middle to low class families who worked dead end jobs.

As I walked, one of the houses came to life. My presence set off the front yard sensor light. Unconsciously, my hand dived into the pocket of my sweater and gripped the handle of the box cutter. I was relieved when no one came out. The first thing I noticed was a blue and white neighborhood crime watch sign hanging off of the fence that surrounded the house. Hanging next to it was another sign with bright orange letters that said 'Forget the dog, Beware of the owner.' Underneath the words was a single hand wrapped around the base of a gun. For some reason, the sight of the sign gave me the chills. The next thought I had was a wish that it was my hand that was holding the gun.

After walking a few more blocks, the scenery and vibe of the night suddenly began to change. I approached an area of the city known as the underworld. The underworld was a part of town that was foreign to me but I heard many stories on the news of how this area was known for prostitution and robbery. I didn't care. For my son, I would walk through fire.

I continued to walk with caution. I ended up on a street that looked like it was a dusty back road deep down in Alabama somewhere. The street lights were so dim that the people I saw in the distance looked like nothing but shadows. A few abandoned cars lined the street. The car closest to me looked as though the torching it suffered was recent. As I approached the car I heard the sound of someone moaning and grunting. I walked with light steps pass the car and what I saw blew my mind. I thought my eyes were deceiving me. Inside of the car, there was a man and woman who was both butt naked. I looked away as fast as I could and tried to hurry pass the car.

I didn't want to be noticed by them but they must've heard my footsteps because they both stopped trying to please each other and looked at me. I sped up my steps and they went back to doing what they were doing as if I was never there. I prayed that R.J. hadn't traveled this far into the city.

The further I walked into the area, the more it came to life. I slowed my pace when I noticed that about eight females were scattered on both sides of the street. It was obvious that I was roaming around in the prostitution section of the underworld. To say that I was nervous would be an understatement. I remembered the box cutter and stuffed my hand into my sweater pocket and clutched on to it. I was still nervous. Where was my baby?

Slowly I rotated my head from left to right in search of any sign of my child. Out of nowhere, a strong voice boomed into the air.

"Whatever it is that you're looking for is not around here so you better be leaving."

I didn't know if the voice belonged to a man or a woman. When I turned my head into the direction of the voice I saw that I was being approached by a very broad shouldered person wearing a pair of baggy jeans and construction boots. I assumed that it was a guy, but it wasn't. The person approaching me was a six foot two hundred and fifty pound bull dike who looked like she could easily put a beating on the average everyday man. I tightened my grip on the box cutter and used my thumb to slide the blade out a little. She stopped directly in front of me. I swallowed what felt like a bowling ball and my reflexes caused me to pull out my weapon.

I slid the blade out as far as it would go.

"Stay back or I'll cut you!"

The bull dike took one step back then started to chuckle. In the blink of an eye, her smile was gone and her face turned to stone. She watched me with evil eyes and placed two fingers into her mouth and whistled so loud that it hurt my ears. The footsteps I heard sounded like a bunch of stampeding horses. I was still pointing the blade at the amazon but when I looked around, I knew I was in trouble. All of the females that lined the street a second ago were now coming towards me and my manly looking enemy.

As they marched towards us, each of them bent down to pick up a weapon. A few of them picked up what looked like broken broom sticks and others had broken glass. I wanted to run but there was nowhere for me to go. When I looked back at the bull dike, I almost peed my pants when I saw that she was now holding a small caliber pistol in her hand. Her face was still as hard as a rock.

"Now what exactly do you plan on doing with that little butter knife?"

She raised the gun and pointed it at my head. I wanted to cry. Her army of streetwalkers surrounded me. In one split second I was able to take in all of their faces. They all looked rough; like they all had seen too many of the horrors life had to offer. I was beyond afraid. Then I remembered R.J... The thought of him being somewhere in danger and in need of my help caused an electric bolt of courage to shoot through my body... They would have to kill me to stop me from walking away and continuing the search for my baby.

I tossed the box cutter to the ground and rolled up the sleeves of my sweater. Next I looked directly into the eyes of the leader of the pack.

"Listen. I didn't do anything to you and I don't want any trouble. The only reason I'm out here is because my ten year old son ran away from home and I'm trying to find him and nothing or no one is going to stop me from getting to my son. If that means that I have to fight each and every one of you to be able to walk away and find my child, than that's exactly what I will do."

The leader just stared at me for a second. It looked like her eyes were softening up. She let the gun fall to her side. Her wolf pack was a different story. They continued to look at me like I was a hunted enemy trapped behind enemy lines. I don't think that they believed my story, or if they did, they just didn't care.

The bull dike looking female cocked her head to the side and looked deep into my face. I guess she was searching for the slightest hint of my story to be untrue. Then from behind me, one of the girls, who looked like she weighed ninety-seven pounds and like she only had about five teeth in her mouth, tried to provoke the situation.

"I think she is lying to us."

The one in charge came stomping towards me. My adrenaline started to pump and I put up my guard. I held my tiny fist up in the air and I know I looked like I didn't have a clue as to what I was doing. I even heard one of the other girls laugh at me. The bull dike lady blew pass me. She stopped in front of the missing tooth girl. The entire crowd took a step backwards. She towered over the toothless girl like a giant over a mouse.

The giant dike brought her face within inches of tiny mouse.

"Who told you to say anything? Did I tell you to speak?"

She stared down at the smaller lady like she dared her to say another word but the smaller lady didn't. She just stood there as stiff as a board. She had the look of a disobedient scared child that didn't want to get hit.

The threatening stare lasted a few seconds then the bull dike turned her head in my direction.

"Get out of here and go and find your son."

She didn't have to tell me twice. The crowd made an opening for me and I exited the circle with caution. I was only about ten steps away from them when I heard the dikes deep voice.

"Hey!"

My body froze and I had to resist the urge to run. Slowly I turned around. The dike was coming towards me.

"Here, you might need this."

She handed me my box cutter and I gladly took it.

"Thank you."

"There's no time to be thanking me. You go and find that precious little boy."

All I could do was nod my head in appreciation. I turned around and continued my search for R.J... Not three minutes passed before the real nightmare began.

I turned the corner onto another deserted street. This one had nobody outside. Out of nowhere, a black car pulled up beside me and two men jumped out of it. One of the men was black and the other one was white. I reached for my weapon but before I could grab my blade, the black man jumped me and tackled me to the ground. I let out a scream. The man who tackled me tightly held my hands behind my back. I struggled, but couldn't move so I screamed at the top of my lungs.

"Let me go!!!"

The white man, who was still standing, raised his foot and kicked me in the side. Excruciating pain shot through me. The white man bent down and spoke to me in a calm voice.

"The more you fight, the worst this is going to be on you."

I didn't know what he meant until the black guy turned me over and reached down to undo my pants. (They were about to rape me). Right there in the middle of the street they were going to rape me.

I struggled and kicked my feet viscously.

"Stop!!! Get off of me!!! Help!!! Somebody help!!!"

The white man slammed his fist into my face. The pain was unbearable and immediately the taste of warm blood filled my mouth. There was no way that I could hold back the tears.

"Please let me go! Please! Let me go! Don't do this to me!!!"

My cries were met with another punch to my face. Then he punched me again and again. The blows to my face were making me weak and I didn't realize it but the black man had somehow pulled not only my jeans but also my panties down to my ankles. With the little bit of strength I had left, I continued to put up a useless fight.

When I felt one of their hands grope my pubic area, I began to cry. Next I felt one of their fingers being forced inside of me, that's when I knew that I could not escape the rape. My bare backside scraped the hard concrete. I was ready to give up but I thought about how much my son needed me and I mustered up the strength to let out one last cry.

"Heeeelp!!!"

Then I heard a gunshot.

"Pow"

Followed by two more.

"Pow" "Pow"

The two would be rapist stopped their attack on me. They jumped up off of me and tripped over each other trying to make it to their vehicle. When I looked up to see who was doing the shooting, I was happy to see that it was the bull dike. She was running towards me with her small gun raised into the air and her posse of street walkers behind her. They had saved me. My tears of fear turned into tears of joy. Then my tears of joy turned into tears of pain because when I stopped my search for R.J., I went home only to find out that he was lying in his bed safe and sound. He had never left the house. After he wrote his runaway letter, he hid himself in his bedroom closet. I could've killed him that night, even worse, that night I could've been killed.

æææææææææææææææææææææææææææ

Valarie closed the diary. R.J. sat there with an overwhelming sense of guilt. He felt like both his wife and his father were looking at him with accusing eyes. He could not look at either of them in the face so he sat back in his seat and closed his eyes.

This was his first time hearing about all of the abuse that his mother suffered because of his selfish prank. Visions of his mother being assaulted flashed through his mind. She was attacked and almost raped and could have even been killed all because he wanted a little bit of attention.

    A terrible storm of guilt swarmed his body. He opened his eyes to see that his wife and father were still quietly watching him. It was obvious that R.J. was in a world of hurt. They let him sit with his thoughts. R.J. looked at his father. His father looked back at him with eyes that did not hold judgement. Seeing the amount of compassion that Randy had glowing in his eyes only made R.J.s guilt trip worse. He looked away from his father in shame In R.J.s mind Randy was no longer the bad guy. Nothing that Randy had ever done was as bad as what Valarie had just read.

    R.J. felt a burning sensation behind his nose and knew that tears were about to fall. He rose up out of his seat and headed for the front door. Valarie got up behind him.

"Are you okay baby?"

R.J. stopped walking and turned towards her.

"Yes, I am okay. Just stay here. I will be right back, I need some fresh air."

"You sure you don't want me to join you?"

"Yeah I'm sure."

    R.J. felt shattered and destroyed. He would never be able to look at himself in the mirror again. He opened the front door and before he stepped out into the hallway he looked at Valarie one last time.

"I will be back in a few minutes, don't worry about me, I will be okay."

Without protest she began to back away from the door. She looked at her husband with sympathetic eyes as he walked out of the door.

R.J. hadn't cried since his mother's death, but once he was alone in the hallway, the stinging feeling in the back of his nose almost forced out a tear. The anger he felt towards himself was the only reason he didn't cry. He balled his fist and was about to punch the hallway wall but stopped because he heard his apartment door open. When he turned around, he saw Randy. Randy closed the door behind him and stood on the welcome mat to R.J.s home.

Their eyes met for a fraction of a second. R.J. unballed his fist and looked away. He started to pace the hallway up and down. Randy watched him. R.J. knew that he would never be the same after finding out about the dangers that his childish ways had caused his mother. How could he have been so selfish? He wished that there was some way for him to apologize to his mother, but there wasn't. She was dead and gone and only the lord knew if he would ever see her again.

He paced to one end of the hall then back down into Randys direction. When he reached Randy he turned and headed back the other way without even looking at him.

Randy cleared his throat.

"Are you okay?"

R.J. stopped in his tracks. Slowly he turned his body into Randy's direction. He was embarrassed and knew that Randy could see that. It hurt him to his heart to let Randy see him in such a weak state but there was nothing he could do about it.

R.J. inhaled deeply.

"I guess I am... I'm just trying to figure some things out."

"So am I"

R.J. was touched by Randy's words. He knew that Randy was crying out to be forgiving. Randy looked into his sons face with pleading eyes that begged for R.J. to understand that some things were just out of their control, and the effect of such things, were effects that no one could do anything about.

At that very moment R.J. understood… and for the first time in his life, although it was only mentally, he made an emotional connection with his father. The mental connection lasted a slight second as they stood in front of R.J.s apartment. The connection could only be described as a father and son moment.

R.J. was already feeling bad about what Valarie had revealed to them but he began to feel worse because he had attacked Randy. They stood there for an emotional moment and Randy was the one to break the silence.

"You didn't do anything wrong. You were just an innocent child who wanted his father. If anyone is to blame, it is me."

"You don't have to do that Randy. You were incarcerated for trying to feed me. I was selfish. I should have waited for you to return. If I would have done that then none of this would have happen."

"Come on R.J., like you told me; don't be so hard on yourself. You were young back then. You weren't the man that you are now. You were only a kid that needed his father and I shouldn't have left you."

Randy's words hurt more than they helped. R.J. found himself feeling that Randy was more of a man than he was being given credit for. R.J. knew that only a true man would sacrifice his own freedom to put food on the table for his family. With that thought, R.J. came to the conclusion that it was also his fault that Randy went away.

R.J. stood there with a broken heart.

"Randy, you went to prison for writing a few bad checks to feed your family. I apologize for the way that I have treated you and for how I rejected you for the past fifteen years. Please forgive me."

Randy looked touched.

"Listen. You don't ever have to ask for my forgiveness. You are my son and just like I would have done anything for you back then, I will do the same thing now."

R.J. didn't respond and Randy didn't say anything else. They stood there lost in their separate thoughts. Each man feeling as though they were to blame for something that neither one of them had any control over. For the first time ever, besides their identical looks, R.J. had something in common with his father.

Suddenly Randy made a swift move. He reached out and embraced R.J. into his arms without giving him a chance to object it. R.J. was taken by surprise. As an adult, he had never hugged his father. Randy squeezed his son tightly.

"Everything is going to be fine R.J… everything is going to be fine."

R.J. stood stiff. He didn't know how to react. His arms hung limp at his side. He felt a re-assuring pat on his back.

"I promise you that we will get through this together."

R.J. lifted his arms and returned the hug to Randy. It felt strange, but also as genuine a hug as any other hug he ever felt.

With his head buried above his father's shoulder he looked at his apartment door and noticed the darkness surrounding the peep hole. Valarie had been watching the two of them the entire time. The peep hole suddenly shone light. She must have realized that she had been spotted. It felt like someone had poured a warm liquid into R.J.s body. He knew that his wife was smiling on the other side of the door so he smiled and tightened his hug on his father.

They unlocked their hold on one another and when R.J. looked at Randy he had a quick vision of a good future relationship with the man.

"How bout we get back to my mother's diary."

Randy looked happy.

"How bout we do it."

In a peaceful silence, R.J. led the way back into the apartment.

Valarie had returned her pregnant body to her seat. She sat in the recliner and looked up at the pair with smiling eyes. She didn't have to say anything but R.J. knew that she was happy for them and proud of him for accepting comfort from his father in his time of need. What Valarie didn't know is that R.J. couldn't wait to tell her how good it felt to finally have experienced what a father and son moment felt like. It was something that he had stopped thinking could happen a long time ago. From the look on Randy's face, the moment they shared was just as appreciated.

Valarie, with much effort, was able to lift her swollen body up out of the chair. She walked over to R.J. and placed a soft kiss on his cheek.

"Is everything okay?"

Before he spoke, R.J. put a loving hand over her swollen belly.

"Yes honey. Everything is fine."

The baby kicked and R.J. reacted like a true first time father to be.

"Did you feel that Valarie! The baby kicked when I touched your stomach."

He bent down and started speaking to her stomach.

"Hey you in there. How are you doing little fella? It's me, daddy."

The baby kicked again.

"He did it again! Did you feel it? He knows it's me!"

Valarie smiled at her husband

"Of course I felt it. I'm the one being kicked silly."

Valarie grabbed his hand and led him over to the sofa and he sat down. Then she handed him the diary.

"I'm going to make some tea, I will be right back."

On her way to the kitchen she stopped in front of Randy, rested her hand on his shoulder and whispered.

"Thank you."

Randy simply nodded his head.

Valarie was in and out of the kitchen in less than ten minutes. She entered the living room carrying a tray with three steaming cups of tea on top of it. R.J. and Randy were sitting on opposite sides of the same sofa. They were engaged in a conversation with the mother's diary in between them on the middle cushion that was reserved for Valarie.

Valarie sat the tray on the coffee table and served tea to both men. She picked up the diary then took her seat. R.J. sipped the lemon flavored tea and looked at his wife in adoration. Valarie picked up her mug of tea, took a sip then placed it back on to the tray. She looked at the diary in her lap then she looked at her husband and his father.

"Would you guys like me to finish reading?"

Simultaneously they both nodded their heads. Valarie opened the diary to the last page that she had read. She turned to the next page and saw that Shirley Ann had drawn a smiley face that wasn't smiling. Instead the circle face wore a frown and had dotted tears under sad eyes. Valarie looked over to the next page and began to read what turned out to be a shattering chapter of R.J.s mother's life…

CHAPTER 5.

 Lately I've been missing Jody. Sometimes I find myself wondering what would have happened if I would have made the decision to move away with him instead of going back to Randy.

 I even saw Jody the other day. But he didn't see me. He was walking into the building that he lived in. I hadn't seen him in a few weeks, ever since I broke off our relationship. He was still looking good. I wanted to call out his name but was afraid that after how I hurt him he might not want to speak to me. What Jody didn't know is that it hurt me to my heart to let him go.

As I watched him from a distance, I had to physically hold myself back from running into the building after him and diving into his familiar arms to let him know how sorry I was for causing him any pain. He probably would've forgiven me but I will never know because when the door closed behind him, I closed my eyes and shed a tear, then I turned and walked away.

Randy was another story altogether.

He had been home for a couple of weeks. Our re-found relationship started out so good to me. But I never knew that loving Randy could be so bad for me. I was honest with him and I told him all about what happen with Jody. He claimed to understand my actions. But he never told me that he knew Jody.

What Randy did for revenge was sick.

I've known Randy since I was a little girl and no one could've paid me to believe that deep down inside, he was a cold hearted monster. He's so cruel to me. He treats me as if he never loved me. As if I am someone whom he truly hates. It didn't matter to him that I was the mother of his children. All I wanted was for him to forgive me and love me like he once did. But he wouldn't.

During the first week of him being home the two of us were inseparable. He had me feeling like a princess in a fairytale. He'd been gone for a whole year and his love for me seemed to have only grown stronger. It was like he wanted me even more than he did when we first fell in love. But he didn't...

When he came home, he didn't have much but every day he promised me the world. He told me that all I had to do was follow his lead and he would show me the way to paradise. I believed him. But what he promised didn't matter to me. I didn't care for the materialistic things. All I wanted was him; all I needed was him. He didn't have to have anything. I would have loved him forever as long as he was good to me. But he insisted that I put my all in to him because he wanted to feel like a man and be the leader. So I followed. Where I ended up was further away from paradise than I had been before he came home. All I could do now is shake my head and blame myself for letting him do all of the horrible things that I allowed him to do to me. But things started out so nice.

Randy and I went for walks every night when he first came home. Sometimes we would just walk and talk about any and everything. And because we didn't have much money we shared everything. We shared soda pops and bags of popcorn but my favorite moments of sharing were when we went to the ice cream parlor and shared a banana split. He knew that I loved bananas and no matter how hard I tried to make him eat one of the bananas he wouldn't. He always let me have both of the bananas in the ice cream bowl. In return, I would let him have the cherry that sat by its self on top of the banana split.

A lot of people don't realize how much good something as small and simple as sharing ice-cream does for a relationship.

But I did. And not only did I realize it, but I also appreciated it.

Our relationship was just flowing. Even after I told him about Jody, things still seemed okay. When I told him about the affair he looked a little hurt but he assured me that he was fine. He told me that he needed a few days to think things over so I backed away and allowed him his space. Then, after three days went by and he hadn't contacted me, I started to get worried. My worry didn't last long. Randy reached out and got in touch with me on the evening of the third day of not seeing him. He called me and shortly after, he was there to pick me up.

When I opened the door and saw him I was completely blown away by his appearance. He was decked out in a brand new three piece dark beige suit with some nice hard bottom shoes to go along with it. He looked so nice and handsome. All I could do was stare at him with a lust that I hadn't had since he'd went away. Not even Jody and all his natural good looks could hold a candle to the man that was my husband. I wondered where he'd gotten the money from to buy the nice clothes so I asked him and he simply told me that he had come across a few dollars. I took his answer and didn't ask him anymore questions. In the back of my mind I hoped to God that he didn't write anymore bad checks. I think that is what he had done but I couldn't bring my self to ask him so I kept my silent prayer to myself and got ready for the evening.

He told me that he wanted to take me out to dinner and afterwards he was going to take me to a motel so that he could make love to me... Boy was I excited. Not only was I excited to see him, I was also excited because we were going to finally have a chance to be alone. Us being alone didn't happen often because of our living arrangements. He lived with his parents and I lived with mine. Actually, we'd only had the chance to be intimate one time since he's been home. I couldn't wait to share the night with him. It only took me twenty minutes to get dressed then me and him were out the door.

Just like any other night with him since he's been home, the night started out beautifully. The dark blue sky was full of stars and the evening air smelled fresh and blew softly. The weather was so nice that instead of taking a taxi, we chose to walk the mile long distance between my house and the small café that I picked out for us to eat at. I chose the small café because even though he told me that he came into some money I still felt the need to be considerate to his pockets. I don't care about how much money he came into, I knew that he didn't have much.

As we walked we talked about everything including the Jody affair. Randy was so understanding and he swore to me that he'd forgiven me. We walked and walked and I fell in love with him over and over again that night.

At the cafe we shared a nice size sandwich and we were truly having fun but our cafe visit was short lived. Although we were enjoying each other, we both were more eager to get the night moving along so that we could enjoy each other behind the door of which ever motel that he was about to take me too.

When we left the cafe, the night was still as beautiful as ever but the desire we had for one another pushed us into a taxi and rushed us over to a motel that Randy had already preregistered a room for us.

We walked through the entrance of the motel lobby hand and hand, arm and arm and with my body snug tightly up against his. He stopped me from walking in the middle of the lobby and placed a soft kiss on my lips. I felt like I was standing on a cloud and I could have melted right then and there in the strength and comfort of his arms.

I looked up into his face.

"Why are you so good to me? What did I do to deserve this Randy"

He looked down at me with a look that I thought was sincere.

"All I want is for you to feel the same as I do."

I thought he meant that he wanted me to see exactly how it feels to be loved, but as I now know, that was definitely not what he meant.

Now that I think back to how he looked when I asked him the question, I should have picked up from the answer he gave me, something wasn't right. His facial expression was full of love but that answer that he gave me was shallow and incomplete.

He sat me down in the lobby and walked over to the front desk. I watched him with the eyes of a woman in love. He spoke shortly to the female clerk before he reached into his pocket and showed her his identification. The pretty young clerk smiled and I felt a sting of jealousy. She must have been satisfied with his credentials because she reached back behind her and grabbed a set of keys then handed them to him. Randy took the keys and walked away from the desk. As he came towards me he smiled a smile that could light up a room.

I rose to my feet but Randy held his index finger up in my direction indicating that he wanted me to stay put. I looked at him curiously as he crossed the lobby. He walked over to a pay phone then picked up the receiver. As he dropped a coin into the phone he looked back at me and smiled. His lips began to move and I wondered who it was on the other end of the line. Who ever it was that he talked with, their conversation was short.

He walked back over to me with the same brilliant smile that he was wearing a few moments earlier. He grabbed me by my hand and led me to the room where we were going to make love to each other for the rest of the night. He even held the door open for me and let me enter before him.

The fresh scent of wild roses filled the air. For the motel to have been an inexpensive one, I had to admit that the room was nice. A flat screen T.V. hung perfectly centered in the middle of the wall; in one of the corners there was a small computer desk with a touch screen computer and keyboard on top of it. The desk was even equipped with speakers. There were nightstands at both sides of the queen size bed and at the top of the bed there was a beautifully polished silver headboard. What I was impressed by the most were the hundreds rose pedals that Randy had spread across the creamy white bed spread.

The room wasn't large; there was only one small closet. Someone else might of thought the room to be uncomfortable, but I loved it. My conclusion was that Randy had done a good job preparing for our night of passion.

When I took off my shoes my feet sunk into the soft black carpet. Before I had the chance to get comfortable randy came over to me and gently grabbed me by the hand. He pulled me into his chest and looked deep into my eyes. I wondered what he was thinking but before I could ask he bent down and placed a soft kiss on my lips. All I felt at that moment was the love that I had for him. I wished that I had never had a relationship with Jody.

Randy led me to the bathroom and when he opened the door I smiled for the hundredth time. A steaming hot bubble bath was waiting for me. Randy slowly undressed me then picked me up into his arms. He held me in the air and looked into my eyes for a while without saying anything. When he was done looking at me, he walked over to the tub and gently placed me into the hot bubbly water. He let me go and I sat back so that the water could cover my entire body up to my neck. My head was the only part of my body extended above water.

I looked up at him and wanted to tell him how much I loved him but he kissed me before I could speak. His kiss was filled with passion. I wrapped my arms around him and closed my eyes. I wanted the moment to last forever but he pulled away from me and told me that he would be back momentarily. I told him that I wanted him to stay with me but he told me that he wanted me to sit alone with my thoughts for a while. He didn't give me a chance to argue; he walked out of the bathroom and closed the door behind him. I sat back in the tub, closed my eyes and just began to let my thoughts run freely. A silhouette of Jody's face popped into my head, but it didn't stay there long. Inside of the moment that I was living in, Jody didn't matter. I knew that making the decision to go back to Randy was the right choice.

By the time I was done with the bath and just as the water started to get cool, Randy reappeared in the bathroom followed by the sound of low music. At first I didn't realize where the music was coming from. I knew that we hadn't brought a radio with us, then I remembered the speakers on the side of the computer.

Randy smiled at me connivingly. I responded with a little naughty smile of my own. He dried my body then led me back into the room where the lights were now dim. A single candle burned with a powerful sweet fire on each of the nightstands. They were vanilla scented and the aroma that the candles gave off mixed well with the scent of the rose pedals.

I had everything I needed. Dim lights; soft music; sweet fire; and the man I loved. For me to even think of asking for more would be nothing but pure greed. *Everything was perfect.*

I felt like I was floating as he led me by the hand over to the bed. He sat me down and knelt down to his knee directly in front of me. His eyes were smiling as he looked up at me. I was intoxicated with a drunken desire for this man. He reached out and touched my hand with a loving impulse. Then he attacked me with a fierce kiss of lust. The kiss was rough but his lips were soft. His force was strong, but the effect was gentle. When he pulled away from me I could barely catch my breath. Slowly he began to undress me and once he had my clothes off the madness started.

It began with him pulling out a pair of handcuffs. I was too drunk with lust to remember where he had pulled them out from. The handcuffs were covered with a cute black fur. They looked more kinky then they did dangerous and they actually turned me on because I found myself having kinky thoughts that I never had.

He brought his body close to mine then whispered into my ear.

"I'm going to handcuff you to the bed rail then I am going to fill you with all of the feelings that you filled me with."

I didn't say a word. I was at his beck and mercy. All I knew was that I wanted him. I needed him. I wished for him to just take me and do with me as he pleased.

He roped the cuffs around one of the metal bars of the bed rail then he lifted both of my arms into the air and cuffed me. I was naked and stretched out flat on my back with a hunger for him that was almost at a climax. Then he whistled and suddenly and without warning, a female jumped out of the little closet that was in the corner.

My soul panicked with fear. I didn't know what was going on. I looked up at Randy as he looked down at me. His eyes no longer held a smile. They looked wicked. It seemed as though a dark shadow had overcome his face.

The lady who jumped from the closet walked over to Randy's side. She only looked at me for a fraction of a second before giving her full attention to my husband. Her face was unknown to me but it was one that I will never ever forget. She leaned into my husband and started to place slow wet kisses on his neck. At the same time she unbuttoned his shirt. Randy did not move, nor did he make any attempt to stop her. He just stood there like an angry statue staring down at me coldly. I couldn't find a word to say but my eyes pleaded for him to please un-cuff me. I tugged at the handcuffs with all of my might in an attempt to free myself but it was useless. I wanted to cry. And as bad as I wanted to scream, something in my heart told me that it wouldn't matter. He was not going to free me. I was a prisoner of whatever he had planned. Then he said something that almost caused my heart to stop beating.

His eyes looked like hot drops of liquid tar and his words sounded like they were being spoken from the darkness of his soul.

"Jody was my best friend while I was incarcerated."

My eyes swelled with horror. I didn't want to believe him. Volcano's of tears were ready to erupt from with-in me. Jody had used me... I shook my head from side to side and a few tears fell. Then I wondered what Randy was about to do to me.

"Randy I didn't know... I swear to you that I didn't know."

His eyes grew colder. The female at his side continued as if nothing was taking place. She undid the last button of Randy's shirt then pulled it from his shoulders. She started kissing him on his chest and she began to touch him in places that I thought belonged to me.

Randy closed his eyes and began to enjoy her pleasures. All I could do was stare at what was taking place. It felt like someone had stuck their hand into my chest and was squeezing my heart. Heavy tears fell from my eyes. My throat was dry as sand but I managed to force out some words in a weak voice.

"I didn't mean to hurt you ... God knows that I never meant to hurt you...I was just lonely... Please forgive me."

He didn't acknowledge my apology. He seemed to speak pass my words.

"I loved you so much Shirley Ann... So much that I gave up my freedom for you... And I didn't care about going to prison because I loved you and I would have done it again... And while I was in prison, all I did was talk about you."

His voice grew with anger.

"I talked to Jody everyday about you! I told him everything there was to know about you! What you liked, what you didn't like! I even showed him pictures of you! How could you do that to me!!!"

"I didn't know any of that Randy; I swear he never told me that he knew you. I swear---"

"You lie!!! You're a liar!!! And I don't care if you knew that I knew him or not!!! You shouldn't have slept with him!!!"

Randy now had tears in his eyes.

"You were mine Shirley Ann!!! Mine!!! I went to prison for you- you were suppose to wait for me!!!"

Randy was right. And I had no defense. All I could do was lay there handcuffed and crying. He looked at me like I was a no good snake then he spit his venom.

"I hate you Shirley Ann... And there is nothing that you will ever be able to do to change that."

Then Randy turned to his lady friend. He kissed her with a kiss that was supposed to have been mines, and then he laid her down beside me. I cried and begged for him to set me free, but he wouldn't. He ignored my cries and forced me to watch as he made love to her the way he was supposed to make love to me... **Valarie closed the diary...**

CHAPTER 6.

Again the living room was covered by an uncomfortable blanket of silence.

R.J.s eyes were locked on the enlarged picture of his mother that hung on the wall. He sympathized with her pain. He could feel both his wife and his father watching him. Neither one of them spoke. They probably thought that he was upset, but strangely enough, he wasn't.

Although he was bothered by the image he had in his head of his mother being handcuffed to a bedpost against her will, it wasn't enough to stir his anger. He didn't feel as though Randy had physically brought harm to her so he felt no reason to act irrational. He wasn't telling his self that he agreed with what Randy had done but it happened when R.J. was a child. Now he was a grown man. Not only that but he was a grown man in love. And for the love that he shared with Valarie, there was no telling how far off the deep end he would go. R.J.

remembered how just earlier he was standing outside of the apartment door with the thought that his wife was cheating. He knew in his heart that had it not been Randy standing there when he opened the door, he probably would be in police custody right now.

R.J. felt Valarie's light hand land on his shoulder. He took his eyes off of the portrait of his mother and met his wife's gaze. She had pity in her eyes. R.J. wondered if her pity was for him or if it as for his mother. It probably was for both.

Randy cleared his throat and R.J. broke his gaze with Valarie and looked towards the man who had held his mother prisoner in a motel room against her will. Randy's face sagged with uncertainty. He looked like he had no idea of what he should be saying at the moment.

R.J. saw Randy's uncomforting look and knew that the man was nervous so he decided to put his father at ease.

"That was pretty mean Randy but who am I to be the judge of what went on during you and my mother's relationship. I mean, it's not like you put your hands on her."

R.J.s eyes darted down to the diary and shot back up to Randy's face. He had a feeling that in that diary somewhere, if they kept reading, eventually they would come upon a chapter where he did put his hands on her.

He stared at his father curiously. His words were calm but seem to somehow still carry a threat.

"Have you ever put your hands on my mother Randy? Because if you did and she wrote about it in that diary I think it's best if we stop reading now before we get to it because I don't think that I am going to take kindly to it when we come upon it."

Randy's face tensed up. He was obviously offended and he spoke surprising words that carried a threat of their own.

"R.J listen, and please listen well. To answer your question, no, I have never put my hands on your mother… My wife… But yeah, we did go through a lot of things. Some things I am ashamed of and others that I'm not, never-the-less… It was me and your mother whom went through those things, not me, your mother and you."

Randy looked at Valarie apologetically. Then down at her pregnant stomach before looking back at R.J.

"The same way that you and your wife are going through things now that will never involve the child she's carrying."

R.J. sat there looking attentively at his father and he listened with respect to the valid point Randy was making. Then in as quick as the next blink of R.J.s eyes, Randy's face completely transformed into an expression that showed he was ready for all-out war if that is what his next words were about to cause. Randy's eyes were two dots of black emptiness and they viciously stalked R.J.s face. A frightening chill crept down R.J.s spine.

"One more thing R.J…"

Randy's voice was low and very deep. His words sounded like they were coming from a place inside of him that R.J. had never known and probably didn't want to know.

"You attacked me and I forgave you. I forgave you because I blame myself for a lot of what's going on. And truthfully, I anticipated your actions. So long before coming here I prepared myself to accept however you were to react by telling myself that I deserved to be the victim of however you felt. I came here unafraid and ready to suffer the consequences of your anger, even if that meant that I had to let you get a little violent… That's why I did little to defend myself when you attacked me earlier today."

Randy looked beyond serious…

"But R.J. please, I'm begging you not to ever put your hands on me again… I'm begging you to take heed to the fact that before anything else I am a man first, just like you are. And not only that Randy junior, but you should also remember that I am your father. And I don't care about what has happened in the past or what will happen in the future… What I'm basically saying is that through it all it would do you a great justice to never forget that I am the one who brought you into this world, and if you ever try to harm me again, I will be the one who takes you out…"

His words didn't sit well with R.J. The way they stared at each other was the same way two boxers did just before the bell rung. R.J. felt disrespected. Randy's words caused R.J. to clench his teeth together. The chill he felt in his spine from

Randy's intimidating look had disappeared and something dangerous now sat in the pit of R.J.s body.

Valarie sat in between the two of them as stiff as a board. R.J. felt like he had the blood of a mighty warrior running through his veins. He was ready for battle. Randy looked just as ready. R.J. was about to say some words that would probably instigate the situation but he saw Valarie's hand move to her big belly. R.J. suddenly thought about the child that he had growing inside of her body. The baby was due to be there any day. R.J.s next thought was of his child trying to harm him. The thought was ugly because he knew that he would never allow his child to disrespect him no matter the circumstances. In the end, no matter how many different ways R.J. looked at the situation, he came to the conclusion that Randy was right.

R.J. swallowed a big gulp of pride. He knew that he had to be the one to wave the white flag of surrender before their next battle became a war. So with his best effort to defuse the bomb that was about to blow he dropped the tight muscles from his face and simple gave Randy a head nod. And to further show Randy that he was in agreement with him, he told him.

"I completely understand Randy."

Valarie showed R.J. another sign of approval by caressing his back and R.J. looked at her like nothing had just happened.

"If you don't mind, can you continue reading my mother's diary?"

Valarie's eyes reached over to Randy and examined him as if she was searching for him to give her a sign on whether or not he wished for her to continue. He nodded his head and just like that, Valarie was back to reading. But by the time she was done, she wished that she had never had anything to do with R.J.s mother's diary…

æææææææææææææææææææææææææææ

The worse decision I ever made in my life was forgiving Randy. He didn't deserve my forgiveness nor did he deserve me; but I gave him both. As it seems, the more I forgive him, the more he hurts me. It's to the point now that the more he hurts me, the more I find myself wishing that he loved me. And Randy was no fool. When he realized that I was allowing him to take advantage of me, he pushed relentlessly to see how far I would let him go. And me being as stupid as I was, I allowed my weakness for him to let him disrespect me with no limits.

In my eyes I was the one who had hurt him by having the affair with Jody so in my mind that gave him the right to hurt me over and over until he felt like we were even. And as crazy as it sounds, the love I have for him is what gives me the strength to endure all of the pain that he dishes out and causes me.

Randy thought of some cruel ways to try to break me down then afterwards he would leave me alone for days on end to build myself back up. Each time I did so gladly with the hopes that he was satisfied with the revenge that he had taken upon me. But each time I was wrong. He was never satisfied no matter how much I hurt.

It got to a point where I could take no more of his cruelty. That's when I began to pray to God for the strength I needed to break away from the miserable love hold Randy had on me. I did not want to love him anymore but it was too late. Randy probably knew that eventually I would get to that point, so he introduced me to something more powerful than his love. Something that would keep me dependent on him no matter how much I hated him or wanted to let him go. It really didn't matter if I wanted him or not; because I now needed him.

Some months have now gone by since he's been home and he appears to be doing okay for himself. He has had a job for a while now and he even managed to save up enough to get himself a small apartment. I was really proud of him because he hasn't fallen off track and he has been doing exactly what he said he would do when he came home. Well, he hasn't been doing exactly what he said he was going to do because when he came home he said that he would get out of his parents house as well as get me and the children out of my parents house. As it is, he has moved into an apartment but he claims that the place is to small for the four of us.

This revenge thing has gotten way out of hand and it kills me to my soul to know that he would turn his back on our children just to try to hurt me but I have to accept it because the fact remains that it was my cheating ways that have caused my two beautiful children to lose out on having a father. And worse than that, because of what Randy has done to me, my children have also lost their mother. To be completely honest, I guess I can't really blame Randy for being so disgusted with me, what I have become is not worthy of company.

He treats me so wrong... But I need Randy more than ever... I need him and he knows it but he is nowhere to be found. It's to a point where the man will not even answer the phone for me and when I go by his apartment he doesn't even answer the door. He just looks through the peephole and screams for me to go away. I cry, but he acts as if he doesn't hear. I hate to beg but I do, and when I do he acts like he doesn't care. He just stands there watching me like he is getting enjoyment out of it. I wish that I had someone to turn to but I don't. The only one I have left to turn to is the Lord. So every night I talk to God, but he don't say nothing back...

CHAPTER 7.

"Shirley Ann Madison!!! What is wrong with you? Just look at you... What happen to my daughter?"

My mother hated what I had become. She constantly told me that she couldn't believe the way I had thrown my life away chasing behind a no good man. My mother and I had one of the best mother and daughter relationships in the world. We were best friends and we could talk to each other about anything. We never had a disagreement that we couldn't fix before things got out of hand... That was months ago. Back before Randy came home.

Now we are at one anothers throat almost every day. We argue back and forth, up and down and from side to side about the downward spiral my life had taken. As much as I tried to defend my actions, in my heart, I knew that she was right. I knew that she was only trying to help and protect me and that I should have been taking heed to the things that she was telling me but I didn't. I was too far gone and I didn't care about nothing or no one except for Randy. All I wanted was Randy.

I was so far gone and wanted him so bad that I ended up doing something that I don't even think God will forgive me for...

It was pouring down raining outside and I was about to leave my mother's house in a blind search for Randy's love. She didn't want me to go. She claimed that she wanted me to stay in the house with my children but that wasn't it. She just didn't want me running outside behind Randy. I completely lost it and she soon found out the hard way that I wasn't about to let anyone, including her, stop me from getting to Randy

With the children locked in their rooms my mother and I argued about me leaving. We shouted at the top of our lungs. She stood there blocking the doorway and she said and tried any and everything to get me to stay; but me staying just wasn't going to happen. The longer she kept me contained, the angrier I became. I screamed and I screamed and I screamed for her to get out of my way but she wouldn't. She was not about to let me leave out of that house.

"Get out of my way! I am grown and you can't make me stay here if I don't want to!"

"Grown! You're not grown! You don't even know what the word means!"

"Just get out of my way and let me go!"

"You're not going anywhere! What is out there for you but trouble?"

"Don't worry about what's out there for me! None of your business! Just get out of my way so I can go!"

"I'm not letting you go anywhere! Do you see how it's storming out there? What's wrong with you? You are going crazy! That no good man you chasing after don't want you anyhow!"

When she said that, I completely lost control of myself. I was blinded by my heart and no longer did I see the lady standing in front of me as my mother. All I saw was someone who was in the way of me being with Randy. The next thing I remember is me picking up a broom stick and cracking it over my mothers' forehead. She fell to the floor with blood leaking down her face. I was glad she fell because if she would not have fallen, I'm certain that I would have continued to swing the broom stick until she did.

I stepped over the very lady who had loved and nurtured me, like she was a complete stranger. As I stormed out of the house, her haunting words echoed behind me.

"You are no longer my child and I don't care what happens to you out there in those disgusting streets... I don't care if you are dying, I don't ever want to see you again!"

Her words meant nothing. I was on my way to be with my husband, Randy.

The thunderstorm had gotten worse. For the fifth time in an hour I tried to call Randy from a pay phone. Each time he answered and once he heard my voice, each time he gave me the same response.

"Don't you come anywhere near me!"

Then he would hang up in my face. I was left with no purpose and no direction.

As streaks of lightning lit up the night sky; and thunderbolts sounded off; like a true fool, I stood there drowning in heavy raindrops with no place to go. I was soaking wet from head to toe and it felt like I was coming down with an instant case of pneumonia. I thought about calling Randy again but I didn't because at the moment I didn't want to feel his rejection so I roamed around aimlessly in the freezing rain for the next hour. Then I thought of a way that might help me get into Randy's apartment. I remembered that the only times that he wasn't completely rejecting me were times when he wanted to have sex with me. Although I was not in the mood for sex, if Randy was, then I had a shot at finding some temporary shelter from the terrible storm that I was caught in. For the next ten minutes or so I roamed around until I came across another pay phone. All I had was fifty cent left to my name so I hoped that my plan worked.

I dropped my only two quarters into the pay phone then I slowly dialed Randy's number. My heart jumped when I heard his voice after the third ring.

"Hello."

"Randy I'm stuck in the rain with nowhere to go can I please come over?"

"Didn't I tell you---"

"I just want you to make love to me. Please Randy, please make love to me."

There was silence. And in that silence I knew that I had won him over. After his silence came his words

"Do what you want to do Shirley Ann."

He slammed the phone down in my ear before I could say anything. I didn't care. All I knew was that I was about to be with the man that I loved, alone in his apartment while it stormed out side. Nothing in the world could be more romantic. Thirty minutes later, I was on his doorstep.

Randy opened the door and just stared at me. Over his shoulder I could hear the voice of a news broadcaster coming from a radio somewhere inside of the apartment. I stood in his doorway looking up at him like I was a lost puppy who needed saving.

Randy's eyes were extremely glassy. The somber look on his face had him looking nothing like his usual self. I wanted to ask him if he was under the influence of something but I didn't want to push any of his buttons so instead of speaking and messing up the moment I stood there shivering in silence. Enough water was dripping off of me to form a small puddle in front of his doorway. I prayed that he wasn't about to once again slam the door in my face.

He walked away from the door leaving it wide open. I took that as my invitation to enter Randy's apartment for the first time. Once I was inside I closed the door behind me and stood there because I wasn't sure of what I should have done next. As I stood there hugging myself to keep warm I let my eyes inspect the inside of Randy's apartment.

The apartment was just as small, if not smaller than what I imagined it would be. The only furniture he had was a white round wooden table that sat next to the kitchen area and a sofa that doubled to a pull-out bed. The sofa bed sat directly in the middle of the small room with the bed stretched out and unmade. The place didn't even have a television and the only view of the outside world came from a small square window that Randy had left partially open. Even from the distance that I stood away from the window, I could still feel the hawking chill stalking me through the cracked open window.

For entertainment there was only the voice of the news broadcaster that I heard when he opened the door. Then, over in the far corner, in what I guessed to be the kitchen area stood a dingy yellow refrigerator. And sitting on top of it was the source of the news casters voice. It was one of those brown clock radios that showed the time in digital red numbers. For a moment I understood why Randy hadn't offered to move the kids into the place.

The air inside of the apartment was stale and the howling wind that the open window offered did little to help air the place out. Randy ignored me as I stood there drowning in my wet clothes. He sat at the small table and his attention was on whatever it was that he had been doing before I got there.

The crying rain beat against the window as I stood there feeling uncertain if I had made the right decision by coming to Randy's house. Never-the-less, I was there.

I stood there feeling stupid. I didn't even know if I should have gotten myself out of the wet clothing or if I should have just stood there until they dripped dry. Randy's lack of acknowledgement towards me let me know that he didn't care one way or the other what I did. His full attention was on something that he was holding in his hand. He was so into what he was doing that it caused me to be curious so I turned my attention to what he was doing. I focused on what it was that he was holding in his hand. At first, I thought my eyes were playing tricks on me because from where I stood it looked as though he was studying a surgical syringe.

I didn't want to believe what I thought I was seeing so I squinted my eyes to get a better look. To say that what I was seeing had left me awe struck would be an understatement. What I didn't want to believe was confirmed. Randy was sitting at his little white table analyzing a hypodermic needle. The kind with the orange bottom. I was baffled to say the least.

I started to run over to Randy and scream into his face 'What are you doing?' but the words stayed stuck in my throat and before I had time to think my next thought, Randy turned his head towards me and locked his eyes on my face. I've seen Randy look other than himself but at the moment he looked unknown and untrustworthy.

Randy rested the hand that held the needle on one knee and his open palm on his other knee. His face was so unfamiliar. A creepy feeling swam through my entire body. My instincts told me to turn around, open the door and to run like I had never run before. Then he spoke and his words shook me out of my frightened daze.

He spoke with calmness but the demand in his voice was clear and evident.

"Come here Shirley Ann."

Without hesitation, but very slowly, I began to move forward. Each step I took was heavier than the one before it.

Randy's eyes followed me closely. His face was dark. As I approached him I was able to put two and two together and came up with the assumption that he was definitely under the influence of something. And with that information, it's safe to say that was the very moment that I became afraid of Randy.

He continued to watch me closely. I sat down in the chair directly in front of him. For the first moment or so he didn't say anything and neither did I. We just sat there trying to figure out what it was that showed on each other's face. Randy cocked his head from one side to the other. I sat as stiff as a board. He let his eyes examine me from head to toe. While he was inspecting me I let my eyes fall to the needle in his hand. I was almost too scared to breath. His silence was killing me. I looked away from the needle and into his face. I wanted to know what he was thinking. I wanted him to say something. Anything; Little did I know what he said next and what I did next, turned out to be the beginning of the end of my life as I knew it. But for the things that was about to take place, I don't blame him. I blame myself.

Randy swallowed so hard that I heard literally heard it. After that, for some strange reason, his face went from looking unknown to looking as gentle as it did the day we got married. I did not understand what was happening.

He reached out and put his hand underneath my chin.

"You look nervous Shirley Ann. Don't be... I'm not going to hurt you... You do know that right?"

His words put me at instant ease. I believed him. Maybe I shouldn't have but I did so I nodded my head. Randy leaned in towards me. My body tensed up not knowing what to expect. Then he placed a soft kiss on my lips. The second our lips touched, my body relaxed and I melted. He hadn't kissed me like that in such a long time. I was like puddy in his hand and at his beck and mercy. Just like that, it seemed as though the man that I so hungered for had return. I felt wanted again; wanted again by the man that I loved.

Randy pulled his face back about three inches away from mines. He looked at me with tender red bloodshot eyes. To me, he didn't look like he was under the influence anymore; he suddenly looked like the man that I knew before his incarceration.

I was still soaking wet and felt like I would be sick. Occasionally a trickle of water from my damp hair ran down my face. Randy reached out and wiped away a cold drop of water as soon as it emerged from the wet roots of my scout. His eyes turned sad and his voice was weak.

"Shirley Ann, I'm sorry... I'm sorry for the way that I have been treating you."

It looked like he was fighting back tears. He hadn't looked so sincere since he'd been home. His words grabbed my soul and moved my heart. I felt like a dark shadow had been removed from over me. I sat there hoping that Randy's cold hearted ways had blown away with that cloud because I truly couldn't take anymore of how he's treated me since he revealed the truth about him and Jody being friends. He'd been nothing but ice cold and distant towards me and because I felt that I was wrong for seeing Jody while he was incarcerated, I willing accepted all the wrong that he was doing to me. I should've given up on our relationship a long time ago, but I didn't. Instead I continuously prayed to God for Randy to one day wake up and realize that I am only human and all I did was make a mistake. I prayed for him to realize that my heart never left him and for him to see that Jody was only a temporary medicine to a sickness that only Randy could cure. I constantly prayed that he would realize these things. And as I sat there looking into Randy's bloodshot eyes, God was finally answering my prayers. My husband was in love with me again... Or at least that is what he led me to believe.

Randy was still holding the needle in his hand. He looked at me with those soft red eyes as if he was begging me to believe everything that he was telling me.

"I'm sorry Shirley Ann and I will never do anything else to hurt you... Do you hear me Shirley Ann? I will never do anything else to hurt you ever again. Okay?"

I nodded my head. I didn't want him to stop speaking. I'd been waiting for this moment for what felt like forever so I wanted to embrace every one of his words.

He looked at me with a tenderness that I had known in our past.

"Do you forgive me Shirley Ann? Please tell me that you forgive me."

"Yes Randy, I do... I really do... I forgive you."

His deep voice was sincere.

"Do you trust me Shirley Ann?"

My light voice was fragile.

"Yes Randy, I trust you."

"Do you love me Shirley Ann?"

"Yes Randy, I love you."

He sat back in the chair that he was sitting in and looked at me with sharp eyes.

"Will you do anything for me?"

"Yes baby, anything... You name it and I will do it... All you have to do is ask me and whatever it is, I will do... Anything Randy, as long as you love me."

He looked down at the table and I followed his eyes. What I saw is what I guessed to be a toothpaste cap. It sat by its self on the round white table.

It was filled with some kind of clear but cloudy liquid. Randy lifted the hand that was holding the syringe and placed the tip of the needle into the cloudy liquid then he looked at me. I was still staring at the needle in wonderment then my eyes slowly looked up to Randy. For a few seconds we sat there with our eyes locked upon each other.

Randy looked tired. Usually his goatee was well kept but at the moment he was in need of a serious grooming. His red eyes sagged heavily and it made him appear to look like he had been through a lot in a short amount of time. As I sat there looking at him I could tell that his pain had been cutting him as deep as my pain had been cutting me. I wondered if he had been hurting for me as much as I had been hurting for him. Then I was swarmed with guilt. The fact of the matter was that it was my fault he looked so worn out and sad. My heart ached for my love. A lump started to grow in my throat and water welled up in the pits of my eyes but I was able to hold back the tears.

When I spoke my voice gave way and cracked.

"I'm sorry I did this to us Randy."

He didn't interrupt me. He just sat there like I had his full attention.

"I never meant to hurt you or hurt us... I'm so sorry Randy."

My tears became too heavy and I could no longer hold them back. As they streamed down my face I felt dribbles of saliva forming at both corners of my mouth and I became hysterical.

"You did nothing wrong! All you were trying to do was put food on the table for the family! Your family! My family! Our family!"

I pouted like a baby...

"Please forgive me Randy! Please love me again! Don't be mad at me! Please! I'll do anything... Just don't take your love from me! Please Randy! Please—"

He reached out and with the hand that wasn't holding the needle, he placed a finger over my mouth to hush me.

"Shhhh... Calm down baby. Calm down... You don't have to cry. I know that I was hard on you but now I realize that you didn't hurt me intentionally. You were just confused. But don't worry; you will never be confused again. Okay?"

I really didn't know where he was going with his conversation but with a face full of tears and his finger still pressed against my lips, I found myself nodding my head up and down for the third time. Then he took his finger away from my mouth and looked directly into my eyes as he spoke.

"I am going to teach you how to love me the way that I love you Shirley Ann."

I was still crying and sniffling and warm salty tears were still crossing my mouth but I had gained a little control of myself.

"Okay Randy... Please teach me how to love you the way that you love me."

"I will sweetheart... I will... All you have to do is follow my lead like I told you to do before, okay?"

At that moment, Randy could've asked me to rob a bank for him and I would have done it.

"Okay Randy, I will."

"Now roll up your sleeve and hand me your arm."

My entire body locked up. Even my tears seemed to pause. I looked down at the needle then up into his face and thought to myself 'I know you don't think that I am about to sit here and let you stick that thing into my arm'. I must've been taking too long to respond to what he had asked me to do because he repeated his self.

"Pull up your sleeve Shirley Ann, and hand me your arm."

He was sitting there with the needle held upright into the air and he stared at it with a look of interest. Then, I guess he was trying to see if the needle was working, because he pressed down on the back of it and made a little of whatever the liquid was shoot out of the tip of it and up into the air. He looked like a trained doctor about to inject a sick patient.

"This will make everything better Shirley Ann... It will make all of your problems go away and make you love me and ways that you never thought possible."

I didn't know what the heck to do. My mind was telling me for the second time that I should jump up and run and never look back, but my heart was telling me to believe what Randy was saying. I wanted to show him that I did love him the way that he loved me and I know it was stupid, but I was willing to do anything to prove it... So I rolled up my sleeve and held my arm out to him.

Randy gripped my tiny wrist with a strong hand and pulled me closer to him. He raised the needle. And as he brought it towards my arm, I resisted the urge to flinch. I didn't want him to think that I was afraid but I guess he must've sensed my unease because he tightened his hold on my wrist. He never looked up at me. His full attention was on one of my veins.

"Just relax Shirley; this is what you have been waiting for all of your life."

I tried to do as I was told but I just couldn't relax. Neither could I continue to keep my eyes open knowing that the syringe was approaching my arm so just before the sharp point of the needle reached me, I slammed my eyes shut. A split second later I felt a soft pinch and I was sure that my skin had been penetrated. My eyes popped open.

Randy was pressing down on the orange back of the needle. I watched as the clear cloudy liquid disappeared into my vein. At first nothing changed. It turned out to be not as bad as I thought it was going to be. I was happy that it was over. I looked into Randy face and smiled. Then from out of nowhere, a very unknown warm sensation began to swim through me. The unknown feeling that started out in the vein of my arm, swiftly traveled through me. The feeling was beautiful to say the least. My whole body was warm but my thoughts weren't. My conscious was trying to tell me that the feeling was cold and ugly. But just as Randy had said, I felt no pain. I felt worry free. I had never in my entire life known relaxation at this level. My conscious tried to tell me that I had never felt such a feeling because I wasn't supposed to. My eyes blinked slowly.

In my heart, I knew that my conscious was right, but at the moment I was not interested in the argument that my conscious put up. I was only interested in the unknown feeling of warm ecstasy that I was experiencing. My eyes were suddenly too heavy for me to hold open. Without my consent my eyelids began to shut down and the world slowly started to fade away.

No matter how hard I tried, I couldn't seem to keep my eyes open. The mysterious feeling of warm pleasure cuddled me into the comfort of its arms. No man had ever embraced me like this before. I wanted to stay wrapped in the feeling forever. I sat there staring at the back of my eyelids. I wasn't sure but I think I felt a smile on my face. I concentrated on opening my eyes but couldn't find the strength. My five senses were scattered and confused by the seductive pleasure of something unknown. I couldn't even speak. I tried to put energy into forming words but it was useless so I turned my attention back to the task of trying to open my eyes. This time I had a little more success.

The invisible force that held my eyelids shut slowly released its hold. At a snail's pace, my lids began to rise only to find out that the struggle to open them was pointless. My vision was but a blur. I could not see anything clearly. Then I heard something but it was too muffled for me to make out what. My sense of hearing was scrambled. My logic told me that the muffled sound was Randy talking. The hazy blur in front of me had to be him. He was trying to say something to me but I couldn't make out his words. I felt myself lean forward.

I wasn't sure because I hadn't given my brain an order to make my body move but I felt like I was rocking back and forth in a nodding motion. I had no control over myself and I must have nodded to far forward because before I knew what was happening, I felt myself falling and the living room floor came crashing into my face.

The slam against my face was hard but I felt no pain. I actually started to laugh then I remember blinking in an attempt to regain myself. The partly open window came into view. The curtains were blowing with the howling wind and the tiny storm of rain drops sounded like meteors crashing against the window. The only other thing that I could hear clearly was the newscaster's voice saying something about how he could report the news of the whole world in ten minutes. I thought to myself that he was exaggerating and I laughed. The scratchy static behind the voice began to sound like an army platoon sending out an s.o.s but it wasn't. What the newscaster now reported was far worst. The newscaster was now speaking about some horrific tragedy that took place at a pre-school. A man armed with some type of army assault rifle opened fire in a classroom killing eighteen children; all of them under the age of five.

    I never came out of that daze and I will never forget about the two tragedies that took place on that day. One being the pre-school shooting, the other, me shooting heroin into my arm...

CHAPTER 8.

When Valarie stopped reading the mother's diary, R.J. was leaned forward with his elbows on his knees and his head hanging between his shoulders. He looked destroyed, like a football player who had just missed the winning touchdown catch.

His thoughts troubled him. The man who had gotten his mother hooked on the drug that led to her death, was sitting right there in his living room with him. R.J. didn't know how to react. The forgiveness that he had granted Randy meant nothing at the moment. For years and years, R.J. had been trying to figure out how and why his mother had gotten turned out on heroin. Finally he had the answer. His mother was introduced to the cause of her death by her own husband and father of her children.

It burned R.J.s soul to learn that Randy was such a heartless monster. His actions were beyond cruel; unforgivable; and warranted extreme punishment. 'How could he be cruel enough to trick his own wife into sticking a needle into her arm?' R.J. came to the conclusion that Randy had taken full advantage of his mother and the love she had for him. His mother had an emptiness that only Randy could have filled, but didn't. Instead of filling his mother's emptiness with love, he chose to fill her with poison. R.J. slowly raised his head and looked pass Valarie at his father.

Randy was already looking at him. The room was quiet. R.J. had a million questions for Randy but because of the boiling anger inside of him; he had no words for the man. Looking at his father made his heart rate speed up. R.J.s mental and emotional being was on the verge of a violent eruption. To say he was mad would be an understatement. Randy had to pay for the role that he played in the cause of his mother's death.

To R.J., Randy had killed her…

R.J. didn't know what to do. He could no longer look the man in the face. With a question mark left hanging in the air, he looked away from Randy and rested his eyes on Valarie, his wife; the love of his life. The sight of Valarie only caused him to feel more displeasure. His horrifying truth had been discovered. Valarie now knew things that R.J. tried so hard to keep from her.

Valarie sat there with the closed diary in her lap. Her eyes were sad. R.J. didn't know if her sad expression was out of sentiment for him and the current situation or if it was out of regret for being the one who narrated the devastating events that transpired in R.J.s mother's life.

R.J. looked into the beautiful eyes of his wife and he thought about how much he loved her. He thought about how he would never do to her the things that his father had done to his mother. He prayed that she didn't see him as being anything like his father.

He felt a sudden urge to re-assure her of the love he had for her.

"I love you Valarie and I have never, and will never, do anything to hurt you."

"I love you to R.J. and I know that you would never hurt me… nor will I ever do anything to hurt you."

"Thank you. I appreciate your words now can you please excuse me so that I can speak with my fath--, with Randy."

She looked shocked by his blunt words and had a look on her face like she was thinking about not leaving the room. R.J. continued to stare at her with a look of impatient patience. Valarie took a deep breath. Then with hesitation and still in possession of the diary, she raised her pregnant body from in between the two men. She never stopped looking at R.J. as she left the room and he never took his eyes off of her.

Once his wife was out of sight, R.J. returned his eyes to Randy. Randy sat there looking lost and full of sorrow but R.J. didn't care.

R.J.s voice was desperately low.

"What were you thinking Randy? Why would you--- How could you do something like that?"

There was a split second of silence. In that split second, R.J.s voice grew dangerously cold.

"Why did you force that needle into my mother's arm?"

Randy shook his head from side to side and the look on his face was one that said he didn't owe R.J. an explanation for his actions.

"R.J., I've already told you. Your mother and I went through a lot of things… Some of those things were good and some of those things were bad."

R.J. felt like Randy was trying to avoid answering the question and it caused his blood to boil hotter and hotter by the second.

Now his voice sounded dangerous.

"Why did you do it Randy?"

Randy burst.

"I don't know! Ok R.J.! I don't know why I did such a thing, but I have asked myself that same question over and over again! A million times! And not only that R.J., but guess what else… I've also thought the same thoughts that you are thinking! I've felt the same way you feel right now! What's wrong with you! Are you forgetting that she was my wife and I loved her! I never meant for this to happen!"

R.J. felt like he had just been hit with a ton of bricks. He couldn't believe the words that had just come out of Randy's mouth. He felt insulted. Randy had to be joking but R.J. wasn't in the least bit amused. Like an angry giant, R.J. slowly rose to his feet.

Randy took pre-caution and rose alongside him. He must've thought that if R.J. attacked him again then he stood a better chance of defending himself if he was on his feet. He looked more prepared than he did in the earlier attack. He looked more ready for war than he did afraid.

R.J. would never consider Randy his father again. He stared at the man with unreadable eyes. All he could think about was how the man had tricked his mother with a promise of love. Randy had told her that he was teaching her how to love him the way that he loved her. R.J. flew into a rage.

"She was your wife! And you know how I feel! What! You loved her!"

"I did!"

The shouting began.

"No you didn't! You didn't love her and you don't know how I feel or what I am thinking right now! What is wrong with me? No, what is wrong with you? Matter of fact, I know what's wrong with you! You're sick! You're sick and you're selfish! Don't you ever say that you love or loved her again! Don't say it!!!"

"I did love her and you can't tell me that I didn't!!!"

"You didn't! And stop saying that you did! Cause if you did loved her you would not have forced that needle into her arm!!!"

"I was young R.J... I was young and I was confused!!!"

"You were stupid Randy! You were stupid and you were selfish!!!"

"I gave her a decision! She could've said no! I didn't force her to do anything!!! She did it because that's what she wanted to do!!!"

An atomic bomb exploded inside of R.J.

"You killed her!!!"

Randy fell speechless and R.J.s voice dropped as he repeated what he believed in his heart to be the truth.

"You killed her Randy... You killed my mother."

A dangerous silence filled the air. R.J. stood about four feet away from Randy with unsteady breathing. Hot angry air caused his chest to inflate up and down. He wanted to attack Randy but a simple beating wouldn't take away the pain that R.J. had in his heart. The hate that he felt at the moment came from the core of his soul. Randy had sentenced his mother to die and R.J. had to have revenge. The murderer had to pay, but to simply do Randy bodily harm wouldn't be enough. He should suffer the same fate that he imposed on the woman who was only asking him to give her love. R.J. thought about the gun that was in the shoe box in the back of his closet. His blood felt like fire in his veins and his heart ached for his mother like never before.

R.J. looked up at the giant portrait of his mother that was hanging in his living room. There was a stinging burn behind his eyes then the tears started to fall. With his tears in his eyes and his eyes still locked on the picture of his mother, R.J. took a step backwards.

Randy braced himself like he was expecting R.J. to charge at him the way that he did earlier in the day, but his son didn't. R.J. just continued to cry as he looked up at the picture of his mother. Then he turned to Randy and looked at him with murder in his eyes.

R.J. took a step away from Randy. Randy looked confused.

"R.J. please, just hear me out."

He ignored Randy. His eyes blinked out tears of revenge. His thoughts were more than dangerous. He easily envisioned himself committing the ultimate sin against his father. R.J. turned his back to Randy and with murderous steps he stomped towards his bedroom.

R.J. burst through the door. Valarie was the first thing to come into view. She was standing in front of the closet door in an attempt to stop the man she loved from doing something that he would regret for the rest of his life. It was obvious that she had over heard the heated exchange that took place between her husband and his father.

With her large stomach poking and her hands behind her back pressed against the closet door, she looked at R.J. with begging eyes. She knew that he was coming for the gun.

"R.J. no.."

R.J. heard his wife's words loud and clear but at the same time he didn't hear her. He had tunnel vision. All he saw was himself getting to the gun. Nothing or no one was gonna stop him from making Randy pay for what he'd done. He continued to step towards the closet. Valarie raised her hands up like she was about to push him.

"Please R.J., I know your mad right now but think. Don't do this baby. Please think. You have to much to lose. Think about me; think about us."

She raised her shirt and exposed her pregnant belly to him.

"Think about the baby R.J. please! We need you!"

R.J. stopped with about one step of space separating him from her.

"Move out of the way Valarie!"

"No R.J. don't do this. I need you. The baby is due any day and he needs you. Please baby, Please."

Tears of blood were still in R.J.s eyes. His thoughts still cloudy. His heart still hurting for his mother. Then he did some things that he would've never done had he been in his right state of mind.

First he screamed at her.

"Valarie I said move!!!"

R.J. took the final step then he raised his hands and pushed his pregnant wife from in front of the closet door. She stumbled to the side and almost tripped over her own feet but somehow managed to prevent herself from falling.

R.J. snatched the closet door open. Valarie burst into tears.

"No R.J.!!! Noooo!!!"

It was to late. R.J. had already snatched the shoe box down off of the shelf. He tore open the box and pulled out a small caliber handgun. The feel of the gun in the palm of his hand caused a blast of adrenaline to shoot through him. He dropped the gun to his side and charged pass his hysterical wife. R.J. shot out into the hallway that led to the living room where Randy was. He was possessed. No words could express the ugliness of R.J.s thoughts. He had suddenly become a wild beast. A wild beast that smelled blood. R.J. took one step into the living room then stopped walking.

The gun was gripped tight in his hand and hung dangerously at his side. He was drunk with hate. When Randy came into view, R.J. saw bloody murder. His eyes stalked his enemy while dropping tears of revenge for his lost mother.

Randy looked down at the gun then back up into his sons crazy eyes. For the first time, Randy truly looked afraid. And at the same time he looked like he knew that being afraid wouldn't save him.

He took a deep breath.

"R.J. I never meant to hurt your mother. I was young and confused and like you said stupid."

R.J. didn't respond. He didn't move. The burning tears continued to fall. He wasn't even paying attention to what Randy had to say. His mind was flooded with visions of his mother and how she suffered in her painful last days. He remembered how no one came to help; he remembered how he wished he could've traded places with her to take away some of her pain. His heart ached like never before. He remembered how sometimes he would leave her alone in her pain because he didn't want her to see him crying.

Now, he stood in his living room crying because he knew who had caused his mother's pain. The burning tears started to feel like fire dripping from his eyes. R.J. knew what he had to do. He had to wash away the pain forever.

R.J. raised the gun and pointed it at Randy. Randy's eyes grew with fear. R.J. stepped towards his father.

"You killed my mother."

"I didn't R.J., I swear I didn't."

"Yes you did!"

"I'm sorry for all of this but I didn't kill her."

R.J. was becoming more upset because of the fact that Randy wouldn't accept responsibility for what he had done. With the barrel of the gun aimed at Randy, R.J. now stood within arm's reach of his mother's murderer. The gun was just inches away from Randy's face. R.J. had never gripped anything the way he gripped the handle of the gun. Randy raised his hands up in the air as if the police had just order for him to freeze.

R.J. screamed.

"You killed her!!!"

The hand holding the gun began to shake.

"I didn't!"

"You did! You killed her! Admit it! Admit that you killed my mother!!!"

The barrel of the gun was now resting on Randy's forehead. R.J. was completely out of his mind.

"Let me hear you say it!!!"

Randy dropped to his knees. His hands still hung in the air. The cold steel of the gun was still pressed against his forehead. Randy looked up into his son's possessed eyes. The man that he had given life to, was about to kill him. Randy eyes quickly watered and his tears started to flow.

They were both crying like crazy.

"I am not going to say that I killed her!"

"Say it!!! Say that it was you that killed her!!!"

R.J. felt himself getting ready to pull the trigger.

"I want to hear you say it!!! I want to hear you say it!!! I want to hear you say it!!!"

'BOOM'

R.J. heard a loud bang. For a second he thought that he had pulled the trigger but he didn't. He was still holding the gun and looking down at Randy. Randy was still crying and claiming that the mother's death was not his fault. Randy pants were wet and a yellow puddle had formed at his knees.

R.J. wondered what the sound was that he had heard. When he turned his head what he saw almost caused his heart to jump out of his chest. His pregnant wife's body was stretched out across the floor. She must've passed out when she saw R.J. holding the gun to Randy's head. The sight caused R.J.s heart to drop and the gun fell from his hand.

"Valarie!!!"

In three long steps R.J. was across the room and knelling down at his wifes side. His adrenaline pumped. He sat down next to her and cradled her head into the protection of his arms.

"Baby wake up… Wake up baby…"

R.J. had already been crying because of the situation concerning his mother but he no longer cried the tears of a killer. Now his tears were falling in hopes of the well-being of his wife and child. Valarie's pregnant body hung limp in his arms. Her head was tilted at an awkward angle. Her eyes were softly closed. R.J. looked at her belly and hoped that the baby was okay. He pulled his helpless wife into his chest and began to rock back and forth as tears of the unthinkable fell from his eyes. R.J. rocked, cried and prayed. He just so happen to look up. Randy was standing in the middle of the living room with the gun hanging down at his side.

Their eyes locked. A stabbing sensation of hate jolted through R.J.s body. For Randy, there was nothing but pure venom in R.J.s heart.

The words were low and strong.

"Get out of my house."

Randy didn't move.

"Is she okay?"

"Get out of my house!!!"

Randy jumped because of the sudden outburst then he took a few slow steps and stopped at the couch. His eyes were still looking into the eyes of his son. He carefully placed the gun on the couch then continued towards the door. His slow movement suggested that he wanted R.J. to say something to stop him from leaving. R.J. didn't. And Randy left without saying another word. R.J. returned his attention back to his wife, and when he did, he got the scare of his life. A small pool of blood had leaked from in between Valarie's legs.

R.J. screamed.

"Valarie!!!"

She showed no sign of life. R.J. gently placed her head onto the floor then he rushed over to the phone and dialed 911. R.J. screamed his emergency into the receiver of the phone and the paramedics was there with-in a matter of minutes.

CHAPTER 9.

Inside of the operating room, there was chaos...

R.J. stood there looking lost and out of place. Valarie was lying on the operating table unconscious. Nurses scrambled about the room shouting medical terms to each other. To R.J. they might as well have been speaking another language.

A doctor stood at Valaries side giving her a visual examination.

"Come on people, she's losing blood fast. She's getting away from us."

The doctor looked up and when he saw R.J. he pulled the white mask off of his face.

"Get that man out of here!"

A nurse rushed over to R.J. and spoke through a blue face mask.

"I'm sorry sir but you can't be in here, you're going to have to leave."

She pushed at R.J. but he hesitated.

"I'm her husband and that's my child that she's carrying."

"I understand that but you're going to have to leave."

"That's my wife and child. I'm not---"

The nurse snatched the blue mask from her face.

"If you don't leave I'm going to have to call security."

R.J.s eyes turned sad and so did the nurses.

"I could only imagine how you feel. But sir, if you want us to do the best job that we can do to save your wife and child, then you're going to have to leave the operating room."

It was hard but R.J. found the strength to leave his wife on the operating table without him by her side. For a few moments he stood outside of the room looking through the small square window but from where he stood he could not see much of what was going on so he walked away from the door with his head hanging down.

æææææææææææææææææææææææææææææææ

The waiting room was the same waiting room that he sat in after he attacked his father. R.J.s body was numb. He knew that it was his fault that his wife now laid in critical condition. He had never been sadder, but he was too weak to cry.

The waiting room was crowded but he felt like he was the only one there. He paced the floor anxiously. Had he not been so upset with Randy, none of this would be happening. The thought of Randy caused him to exhale deeply. R.J. had almost killed a man. And he would have had Valarie not come into the room and collapsed when she did.

Valarie had saved Randy's life. As a result, she was on the verge of losing her own life, and not only hers, but her child's as well. It was as if she had jumped in front of the gun and bit the bullet for Randy.

'Lord please help me' R.J. thought to himself.

Forty-five minutes later, R.J. was sitting down when the same nurse that had asked him to leave the operating room came rushing through the double doors. R.J. jumped to his feet.

The nurse was looking directly at him over her mask. R.J. felt a fear that he didn't want to feel. The nurse took the final steps towards him. As fast as she was moving, the news had to be bad.

She stopped in front of him then pulled down her mask. She was smiling.

"Your wife is okay and so is your new born."

R.J. dropped to his knees. He felt like the Lord had answered his prayers.

"Thank you lord… thank you… thank you… thank you…"

Then he reached out and grabbed the bottom of the nurses shirt as tears of joy ran down his cheeks.

"Thank you… thank you… thank you… Thank you so much, I owe you my life."

The nurse looked flattered but embarrassed at the same time. She grabbed R.J. by both hands and guided him to his feet.

"You're welcome sir but I am only a nurse. It is the doctor who you should be thanking. He's the one who was able to stop the hemorrhaging and perform the emergency C-section successfully."

R.J. felt gratitude for the man who had ordered him to leave the room. He wiped at his eyes with the bottom of both palms of his hands.

"Are they really okay?"

"Yes sir they really are okay. They are also in the same room but your wife is recovering and she is probably asleep. You can see her but you can't for any reason wake her up. Now you can follow me and I will show you the way to your beautiful new son. Would you like that?"

"Yes ma'am I would."

"Well like I said, just follow me."

Valarie had a healthy baby boy, who was born at six pounds, three ounces. The baby came into the world already sporting a full head of hair and he was the spitting image of R.J. The baby's name was Andy James or A.J. for short. The name Andy was a combination of the name Ann and Randy. Valarie knew how much R.J. loved his mother so she thought it would be nice to combine the two names. R.J. was pleased to say the least.

Valarie laid in the hospital bed resting peacefully and his new born son slept calmly in the incubator right at Valarie's bedside. The room was quiet except for the occasional beep made by one of the many machines that monitored both Valarie and the baby.

R.J. was positioned on the same side of the bed as the incubator. He looked down at his son then over to his wife. He dropped his chin into his chest and shook his head from side to side. He'd never been more ashamed of himself.

In an attempt to avenge the loss of his mother, R.J. had almost lost not only his wife but also his child. He wondered if Valarie was going to ever forgive him.

To see her laying there with all the different medical devices attached to her body made his soul weep. He extended his arm and lightly touched her hand.

"I'm sorry Valarie."

Valarie's hand jerked away from his and the machine did a double beep. R.J. wondered if she had heard him or if she was just aware of his presence. He also wondered why her hand had jerked away from his. He reached out and touched her hand again but she didn't move.

The baby let out a cry. It was the first sound that R.J. ever heard his son make. For no apparent reason, he felt like a proud father. R.J. watched in admiration as Andy whined and moved his tiny arms and legs. Seconds later, the baby was back in a calm sleep. Andy was the seed that R.J. had planted into this world. R.J.s soul was arrested in wonder. He couldn't believe that he was actually looking at a little person that he had created. He looked up at the ceiling and thanked the Lord for allowing his son's safe arrival into the world. When R.J. brought his eyes down from the ceiling and back to his child he had a sudden vision of the boy being a grown man and trying to attack him. The thought made him shiver. R.J. was so caught up in the miracle of his son that he didn't notice that Valaries eyes were watching him.

Her voice was fragile.

"Where's Randy?"

R.J. was startled. He looked over to his wife and became so excited that he had to stop himself from jumping into the bed with her. He swiftly moved around the incubator.

"Baby…"

He was about to lean in and place a kiss on her cheek but the look in her eyes made him second guess the idea. She looked like she was in fear of the fact that her husband might have just commited murder.

"R.J. where is Randy?"

R.J. leaned back up into a standing position.

"I told him to leave the house and to never return."

She smiled and looked relieved that her husband hadn't shot his father. The smile was weak.

"So how does it feel to be a father? Daddy?"

R.J. smiled back at her. His smile was also weak. There was no denying the cloud that hung over them.

"It feels great... It really does... It feels great..."

R.J. eased onto the bed and sat next to his wife.

"Are you okay Valarie?"

She closed her eyes for a few seconds and while her eyes were closed, she shook her head from side to side indicating that she wasn't okay. Then she re-opened her eyes. When she did, R.J. saw unease in them. She seemed to be watching him as if she was in the presence of a snake. The look in her eyes let him know that he could evade her no longer. It was time to face the music. He had to give her some answers but he had no idea of what to say so he decided to wait for her to start asking questions before he ended up opening his mouth and saying the wrong thing. He thought it best to avoid the unavoidable confrontation for as long as he could.

"So how does it feel to be a mother?"

It looked like she didn't want to answer but she did. First she let out a small sigh of what had to be relief.

"How does it feel? It hurts."

They shared a small laugh.

R.J. was consistent in his attempt to stay away from the fire. He looked at his wife with as much a loving look as he could form his face into.

"Thank you for my child Valarie."

He leaned towards her and tried to place a kiss on her forehead but she turned her head away from him. R.J. reacted as if he didn't understand her reason for rejecting him.

"What's the matter?"

She didn't respond.

They were supposed to be sharing the happiest moment of their relationship. They weren't. Valarie continued to look away from him. R.J. was trying to carry on like nothing had happen but deep down inside, he knew he deserved the treatment that he was receiving. He didn't know what else to do so he continued to press his luck.

He reached out and softly placed a finger against the side of Valarie's chin. Gently, he turned her head towards him. The wells of Valarie's eyes were filled to the brim with held back tears.

Something tugged at R.J.s heart. His words sounded innocent.

"What is it baby? What is the matter?"

His voice caused her tears to fall. She looked very unsure and a little afraid to talk but she managed to speak anyway.

"It's you R.J., you are what's wrong."

Her words cut him to the bone. And the way she laid on the bed looking up at him through those glassy eyes made him feel even worse.

"I don't know who you are R.J."

R.J.s thoughts were suddenly dry and his words came out sounding hoarse.

"Yes you do baby… you've always known me."

"No I don't R.J., and I don't even think that you know yourself."

She continued to cry as she searched his face. Then she reminded him of the sad truth.

"First you attack your father R.J., and then you put a gun to his head. And then… and then…"

She was having trouble speaking but somehow managed to get the words out.

"And then you almost kill me and the baby."

She laid there and put her hands over her face to try to hide her tears. R.J. stood there feeling sad and stupid. All he could think of was that he had to comfort her. He reached out and tried to embrace her into his arms.

"I'm sorry Valar---"

When she felt his touch she jumped in disgust and pushed him away.

"Don't touch me! Please Do not touch me."

R.J. backed away from her with a chest full of resentment. What he said to her next was a cry out for her to understand his pain.

"I never meant to put you or the baby at risk. I swear I didn't. You have to believe me. It's just that when I found out about those things that Randy did to my mother, something came over me and I lost it… please forgive me."

"R.J. you did more than just lose control. You almost murdered someone. Now you're sitting here as if nothing has happened.."

Valarie's tears were thick.

"I mean, what happened to your mother is sad. It truly is… but R.J., those things were between her and your father. I know it was a lot to take in but I don't think you should have wanted to kill him. For Christ sake, you weren't even supposed to find out anything about any of it."

The mention of his mother and father in the same sentence reminded him of the hate that he felt for Randy. His thoughts were suddenly black and unconsciously his fist formed a tight ball. Valarie noticed it.

"Look at you R.J… look at the hate that you have in your eyes. You can barely control your anger."

R.J. jumped up off of the hospital bed. Valarie was right about him not being able to control himself when he thought about what Randy had done. There was no reason to lie or to try to hide it any longer. He took steps in one direction of the room then swiftly turned back into the other direction.

R.J. over looked the tears in his Valarie's eyes and for the first time since Randy showed up, he felt the need to be honest with his wife.

"I hate him Valarie!!! I hate him with every ounce of blood that runs through my veins."

He stood there with no love in his heart and spoke truthfully but caught himself in med sentence as if he did care about the consequences of his words.

"Had you not come into that living room when you did---"

The statement didn't need finishing. R.J. stared at his wife with the confession of an awful horror in his eyes. Valarie's face was still wet with tears.

"Say it R.J.! Say that you would've shot him. That's what you wanted to do right? That is what would have made you feel good right? Right R.J.? But let me be the first to tell you... It might've made you feel good, but you would have been wrong."

He couldn't believe that she was siding with Randy again. He stood there feeling like she had said something against him. R.J. watched her slow tears fall and he could tell that her eyes were desperately pleading for him to understand what she was trying to say. He felt like no matter the situation, she should be siding with him. That is what he would've done for her so he didn't want to understand her point. She should be the one understanding him. Slowly he approached her bedside.

His body language must've seemed threatening to her because she looked intimidated. His large frame towered over her.

"What do you mean I would've been wrong?"

"I'm so sorry about all of this R.J. and I completely sympathize with your pain, both yours and your mothers but Randy didn't kill your mother."

Her words stabbed him.

A terrible feeling came over him. He didn't want to believe what his wife was implying.

"What are you trying to say Valarie? You're the one who read the diary. You know as well as I do that if it wasn't for him she would have never stuck that needle into her arm."

"Maybe you're right. Maybe she wouldn't have... but she did. And guess what R.J.? It was her choice."

R.J. voice became heated.

"It was not her choice! He tricked her with the promise of love!"

Valarie popped up into a sitting position.

"He didn't trick her! She was grown! She could've said no!!!"

"She couldn't say no! She was in love!!!"

"And so am I! I am also in love! I am in love with you with all of my heart and soul! But I don't love you enough to stick a needle into my arm! And if you ever asked me to do that, then I would make a choice to get as far away from you as possible! Your mother could have made that same choice!"

"He killed her!!!"

"No he didn't!!!"

"Yes he did!!!"

Their shouts had to be heard out in the hospitals hallway because the nurse came running into the room. The nurse stopped in mid step and looked at the couple cautiously.

"Is everything alright in here?"

Her question hung in the air. R.J. stood over Valarie fueled by anger. He looked down at her with fire in his eyes. Valarie wasn't backing down from him. She sat there and stared at him with eyes full of the same flames that he felt. R.J. didn't like it but he knew that she stood firmly behind every word that she had spoken. He felt betrayed. All he could do was think about his mother. His mother was the only other person who knew and understood; nobody else cared.

Valarie slowly turned her head away from him and looked at the nurse.

"Yes. Everything is okay."

Then she looked back at her husband who had never taken his eyes off of her. The nurse, who just so happened to be the same nurse who had shown R.J. a bit of compassion a while earlier, seemed to have no more pity for him. She slid in between the couple with her back to R.J. and laid Valarie down. Then she began to fix the sheets and without turning around, the nurse spoke to him.

"I think your wife needs some rest sir."

R.J. didn't respond and the nurse must've felt like he wasn't moving fast enough. She quickly spun around and looked directly into his face.

"I am going to have to ask you to leave… again."

R.J. still didn't respond. The nurse was standing there like she was a guard on post to protect Valarie but to R.J. she didn't exist. He continued to stand there and exchange dangerous stares with his wife for a few seconds longer. In the heat of the moment, all he could do was shake his head.

Without saying a word, he turned and headed for the door. Valarie called out to him.

Her voice was soft.

"R.J..."

He wanted to stop, but didn't. Nor did he want to leave his wife and newborn alone with that nurse, but he did. When R.J. entered the waiting room area he didn't even think about having a seat. He exited the hospital like there was nothing in the building that belonged to him.

He stood in the middle of the parking lot. His mind was stuck on one person; Randy. After so many years of absence, why did he have to appear out of thin air? Not only that, but why had he brought with him, the answers to why and how his mother's death came about. R.J. called a taxi and headed for his house.

For the first couple of minutes his conscious ate at him for leaving behind Valarie and their newborn child then his conscious tore at him more for not having what it took to pull that trigger and give Randy what he deserved; a bullet in the face.

The taxi ride home was mental torture. His hate for Randy consumed his mind. He realized that a lot of bitter feelings that he had for the man came from the fact that the man had never been a father to him. Regardless of whatever it was that went on between his two parents as a couple, the two of them still had a duty towards him to up hold. And Randy didn't do the right thing; therefore he had cheated R.J. out of a proper childhood. Although R.J. could have found it with-in himself to forgive Randy for not being a dad, he chose not to. Instead, R.J. decided to use any and every one of Randy's faults as fuel to enhance the flames of hate that he had for the man.

R.J. was mad at himself for even entertaining the thought of forgiveness. How could he forgive Randy for not being there for his mother when in fact he was the one who had caused all of the suffering? He would always hate him for that. Forever; as he had been doing so for the past fifteen years.

But now things had changed…

Before Randy's magical appearance, to R.J., he was out of sight and out of mind. And that allowed R.J. to hate him from a distance and in silence. The distance between them even made it possible for R.J. to hide the hate. But now, with Randy coming back into his life, he could no longer hide his feelings or keep them silent. His hate spoke in volumes and would forever be heard, especially after finding out the truth about the role that Randy played in not only his mother's life but also the role he played in her death.

R.J. couldn't stop being mad at himself for having the opportunity to hate Randy up close and personal and not doing anything to Randy for what he had done to his mother. But one thing was certain. There was no doubt in his mind of what he would do to Randy if he ever saw him again.

When R.J. got out of the taxi he thought about all of the things that Valarie now knew. How was he going to explain all of the things that he purposely kept from her? She probably looked at him like he was a lying monster but little did she know, the darkest secret had yet to be revealed. The secret that was the real cause of R.J.s hate. R.J. had gotten rid of Randy so he was certain that she would never find out what the darkest secret of all was.

R.J. approached the door of his apartment and pulled the keys from his pocket. He tried to place the key into the lock but his shaking hand wouldn't allow him to do so. He snatched the key away from the lock and kicked the bottom of the door. A vision of Valarie and Andy popped into his head and he kicked the door two more times. Then he took the bottom of his fist and pounded it against the door and screamed.

"Why me!!!"

R.J. realized that he was losing control of himself. In an effort to calm himself he rested his head against the door and let out a hard built up breath.

A few seconds passed before he was calm enough to stick the key into the lock. He pushed open the door then slammed it shut behind him.

R.J.s mind was a roller-coaster of conflicting emotions. He walked over to his sofa and sat down. His eyes automatically shut. Guilt and regret had the best of him. How could he be so selfish that he would leave his wife and newborn baby alone in the hospital? He was able to justify his actions by reminding himself that the nurse had told him to leave.

R.J. was truly confused.

His next thought was of Valarie sitting up in that hospital bed crying and arguing with him. He was disappointed beyond belief. How could she argue the side of the man who had caused his mother's death? The man that he so hated.

R.J. lived his life for Valarie. His every action was done in hopes of putting a smile on the lady that he loved face. He lived for her and he would just as quickly die for her. How could she have been so blind and insensitive to R.J.s feelings? For the first time ever, R.J. felt separated from Valarie. He felt like he was all by himself in the world. He hadn't felt so alone since the death of his mother.

R.J. missed his mother so much…

What gave Valarie the right to say that all Randy did was make a mistake? Who did she think she was? How could she expect him to forgive his father? To R.J., Randy was the grim reaper. The man caused death. He would never forgive his so called father and that was all there was to it. It was forgiveness enough that he allowed Randy to walk out of the door in one piece. The loud thumping of R.J.s heart vibrated in the temples of his head in the form of a migraine headache.

He dragged his hand down his face and opened his eyes. The first thing he saw was the large portrait of his mother. The eyes of the picture watched him closely. He knew that he had failed her. How could he look her in the face? He turned his head away from the picture, tightened his fist and slammed it against his knee. His temples pumped louder. R.J. had to do something and he knew what it was.

He had to march back down to the hospital and let Valarie know just how wrong he thought she was.

R.J. jumped up off of the sofa and charged for the door. Just before he reached out to grab the door knob, he felt something underneath his foot and almost slipped but caught his balance. When he looked down, he saw his mothers' diary spread open on the floor. With the reflexes of a cat, R.J. bent down and scooped the diary up into the protection of his hands. A strange feeling came over him. He looked down at the diary, then up at to the large portrait of his mother. The white dress that she wore for some reason appeared to be brighter than usual and the eyes of the picture seemed to be watching him closer. R.J. felt a sudden explosion on the inside that kicked his emotional roller coaster ride in to a higher gear.

The first image that he saw was of Randy; the man was his father. He'd done wrong, but from what it seemed, he was aware of R.J.s feelings of anger and he still came around and endured whatever R.J. dished out. It was as if he was almost willing to lose his life to make amends with his son.

Then he saw a vision of Rachel; his sister. Why was he even upset with her? She deserved forgiveness. Back when all of the madness and sadness was taking place, she was two years older than him but still in all she was only a child herself. It wasn't her fault that her grandmother kept her away when R.J. and their mother needed help besides, she was a kid herself, what could she have really done.

Then he saw Valarie; his friend; his lover; and his world. She had been nothing but loyal and honest to him and she deserved the same in return, but what did R.J. give her but lies? She was the best thing to ever happen to him and he was probably about to lose her because he was a coward. A coward that kept from her things he was so embarrassed about that he thought it would be better to hide it from her rather than to just tell her the truth.

The next vision Randy had was of Andy; his son. The child needed him more than anything in the world and R.J. knew it. But what had R.J. to really offer the child. R.J. was his father and as part of his duties to the child, he was supposed to instill qualities in the child that the child could proudly stand on. Qualities such as Integrity; trust; respect; and honesty. But how could R.J. fill the child with these things if he didn't have them with-in himself to teach.

The final vision R.J. had was of Shirley Ann; his mother. The lady was dead and gone and no matter how bad R.J. wanted her too or what he did, he could not bring her back from the dead. She probably was looking down on him more upset with him than she had ever been before. If not for himself, than at least for her, he had to make things right. With that thought, R.J. suddenly felt at ease like the whole world had just been lifted from his shoulders. A chill shot down his spine and he could feel his mother's presence in the apartment with him.

He looked into the eyes of the portrait of his mother.

"Why mommy? Why did all of this have to happen?"

R.J. felt something crawling on the hand that he was holding the diary in. He looked down and when he did he saw a pretty little red lady bug crawling down his finger, off of his hand, and onto his mother's diary.

When the pretty red bug reached the word Diamond on the diary, it paused for a second, spread its wings and then flew away. He wondered if the ladybug was some type of sign from his mother.

R.J had heard of strange encounters of people claiming to have met with the other side and he wondered if that is what had just taken place. Next he wondered if he was going slapnut crazy.

A smile crossed his face and he let out a much needed laugh. Then he looked up at the ceiling.

"God is good all of the time."

Was all he could think of to say…

R.J. cuffed his mother's diary underneath his arm and headed for the hospital. It was time for him to open up and to tell Valarie the rest of the story. He felt as though it was his duty to tell her about the dark secret. Even if she decided to leave him after he told her, it was still his duty as a man to tell her what happened in his past.

As he walked out of the door he came to the conclusion that it didn't matter what happened after he got to the hospital. What mattered was that he was there.

CHAPTER 10.

    Valarie was standing over the incubator watching Andy sleep. R.J. stood outside of the hospital room door looking through the small square window nervous about entering the room. He knew that once he walked in and told her what he had to say, there was a chance that she would leave him for good.

    He stood outside of the door holding his mother's diary at his side as he adored his wife. She had on a traditional blue hospital gown and

    She looked a little fatigued from just have given birth and her hair was a hot mess but to R.J. she was the most beautiful girl in the entire world. R.J. wondered how long it would be before she returned to her normal size. He loved her figure and hadn't seen it in over nine months. He found himself standing there lusting after his wife.

He wanted his wife. His attraction for her got the best of him and he found himself thinking a bunch of thoughts that were definitely inappropriate at the moment. He pushed the thoughts from his mind but continued to observe Valarie. He could've stood there and watched his lovely wife for days on end. R.J. tried to ease the door open but she sensed his presence and lifted her head in his direction.

They just stared. Their need for one another showed in both of their eyes. For a few seconds, they were completely lost in each other's gaze. R.J. expected for her to be upset but instead she looked worn with worry and in need of her husband. Valarie forced a smile that looked like it could be easily broken. The smile melted away any ice that R.J. may have had left around his heart. Then she said something that sent R.J. flying across the room.

Her voice was a soft whisper.

"Do you ever get the urge to be hugged?"

The question was one that R.J. had asked her a time ago; a time when she really needed him. The question was the first thing to come to his mind on that day when she broke down and confessed to him all of the verbal and mental abuse her uncle had put her through.

R.J. rushed across the room and wrapped his wife into his arms. She was his best friend and she needed him. While embracing her, he realized just how selfish he had been towards her. Somehow, during all of the confusion, he had forgotten that her feelings were wrapped up in this mess as much as his was.

Valarie welcomed R.J.s offer of a truce by resting her head on his shoulder.

"R.J. what has happened to you?"

"I don't know baby... I don't know..."

But he did know. He knew that in the blink of an eye he had turned from a fairytale husband to a stranger from a nightmare.

R.J. didn't want to lose her. He had to re-assure her of the fact that he was still the man that she fell in love with. R.J. released the embrace he had her in just long enough to place is mothers diary down onto the bed. He returned his arms to her body and squeezed her tighter than he did with the first hug.

She took a deep breath. As R.J. held her, he remembered the vow he made to always keep her safe and secure. He knew that this was one moment when she needed re-assuring, of the safety he offered, like never before.

With his left hand he stroked her wild hair.

"It's okay honey. I didn't mean to worry you. I know everything is messed up but it's not as bad as it seems."

"Yes it is R.J."

She backed out of his arms and took a piece of his heart with her. Her sad eyes looked up into his face. He stood there with empty open arms.

"Valarie, I'm asking you to trust me. Everything is okay."

She looked like she was about to respond but caught herself before she started to speak. She looked deep into his eyes then turned her head away from him.

R.J. wondered if he had scared her away from being able to talk to him and he repeated his words.

"Everything is okay Valarie."

"Everything is not okay R.J., it's really not. You scared me. And now I am afraid of you and I don't like that."

"I'm sorry... I didn't mean to scare you... I just---"

"You just what? What R.J.? Pretended to be a saint full of love when the truth is that you are a demon full of hate?"

R.J. wished that she would have a little bit more understanding. His actions might have been extreme but to say that he was a demon full of hate was a bit much.

He denied the accusation.

"That's not true Valarie. I am not full of hate."

"It is true R.J... it is... it is... it is... I don't know who you are... I really don't know you... In my head I thought that you were the perfect gentlemen but in reality you're not. In reality you are capable of doing things. Things that I thought only happen on the news... And R.J.—"

She looked deep into him before she finished.

"R.J. I'm more afraid of you than I was of my uncle. At least I knew what to expect from him. With you, I don't know what's going to happen."

R.J.s voice, which was usually strong, had suddenly shrunk to a barely audible sound as if he himself was unsure of the words that he spoke.

"But you do know me Valarie; and you also know that I will never do anything to harm you."

Her eyes fell to the floor.

"Valarie, you do know that don't you?"

With her eyes still avoiding his, she shook her head from side to side.

"I don't want to be a news story R.J., I don't want who I think you have become... I want the man that I fell in love with."

He closed the small distance between them and grabbed one of her hands.

"Please, just try to understand my anger."

"No... I don't want too."

"I would never harm you."

"I don't know that."

R.J.s suddenly sounded bothered.

"For crying out loud, I just found out that my father killed my mother… What are you going to do? Chop my head off because I'm upset about it?"

She snatched her hand away from his.

"Stop saying that! R.J., he didn't kill her. What he did was give her a choice… the exact same thing that you didn't give me."

She turned her back to him and faced their child. R.J. was baffled. He wondered what choice he hadn't given her.

"What are you talking about? What do you mean I didn't give you a choice?"

She snapped her head back towards him.

"You didn't give me a choice! You say that your father tricked your mother and you're mad at him for doing it but you did the same thing to me."

"I tricked you? How?"

"By pretending to be someone that you weren't"

Her eyes flew a mile pass sad.

"When we got together R.J., I opened up to you and told you everything about me; what I liked and didn't like; my strengths, my fears; about my childhood; and although I had never told anyone, I even told you about all of the ugly things that my uncle Cory had done to me... You found out everything that you needed to know about me then you turned around and used the information against me to make me fall in love with you... I trusted you. But you hid the truth about yourself from me."

She was right and there was no justifying what he had done. All he could do was stand there and listen as she vented her frustrations.

"You never told me about your dark side. Or showed me any sighs that you were capable of murdering someone, and not just anyone, but your own father. Had I know these things—"

Her words drifted. She returned her eyes to their newborn that was sleeping peacefully.

"Had I known these things, I think I'm one hundred percent certain that we would not be here together right now."

She turned her attention back to R.J.

"And don't take this the wrong way, but I would have made the decision your mother should've made. I would have left you alone... Now I'm stuck with a child by a man that I don't even know."

R.J.s heart stopped… then it began to beat again. He felt like his wife had just handed him a black rose. She was killing him softly with her words. But she was so right. And by keeping the truth about his family from her, he had been living a lie the entire three years they had been together. R.J.s shoulders hunched as he walked over to the window. His over confident strut was gone. He moped away and left her standing alone next to their child.

The window had a view of the hospitals parking lot. R.J.s mind was at a standstill. He had lied and she found out the truth. The truth of many dark secrets; but there was still one left. And the secret that was left was the darkest secret of them all. Not only that, but the last secret that R.J. was holding on too was the one that might be able to add some clarity to why he was so upset; but if he revealed it, there was a chance that he might lose her.

He weighed his options and came to the conclusion that he had to take that chance. It was time to tell Valarie what that secret was. He couldn't risk losing his wife under the pretenses that he was just some nutcase who couldn't control his own anger. If he told her and she left than at least he would have a clear conscious.

R.J. looked at Valarie and the next thing he knew, he was on the verge of telling her something that no one else in the living world knew. The only other person that knew what R.J. had covered up inside of him was his mother. And she took the secret to the grave with her. The dark secret was on the tip of his tongue begging to jump off.

"I'm sorry that you had to find out about all of this the way that you did. I am also sorry for the way that you feel, but you wouldn't understand."

He turned his head back towards the window and stared blankly out into the parking lot. His mind began to haunt him for the role that he played in his mother's death. He started to think twice about telling her. Then he felt her approaching from behind.

She gently grabbed his hand and turned him around until he was facing her.

"You say I wouldn't understand, but you will never know unless you give me a chance too. I am here for you R.J., I have always been here. You can talk to me, what is wrong? What are you not telling me.?"

An all too clear vision of his mother lying on her death bed flashed through R.J.s mind. He wanted to tell Valarie what happened. He looked deep into her beautiful brown eyes and saw the same concern and understanding that was always there. He knew that he could trust her and he so desperately wanted to open up to her but he was afraid. Afraid that she would judge him. Not only that but she would also tell him that what he did was wrong; but it wasn't. R.J. was only doing what he had to do. He felt like anybody in the situation that he was in would have done the same thing. The secret was right there ready to be told; but R.J. couldn't find the strength to speak. Valarie folded both of her hands around one of his.

They stood there looking exactly as they did when they stood in front of the pastor at the alter. Back when he made his vows to have her and to hold her; to love her and to trust her. And he did both love her and trust her, he just couldn't find the strength to tell her about what happen between him and his mother.

With a loving pull, Valarie pulled at his arm.

"What R.J.? What is it? What do you have bottled up inside of you? I'm begging you to tell me. Please don't leave me in the dark any longer. I don't want to go on feeling like I share a bed with someone who has the ability to hurt or kill me if I say or do the wrong thing. I don't want to continue to wonder if I should just break off what we have and leave you."

She looked up at him with a face full of doubt. Her words as true as they could have ever been.

"You claim that you would never hurt me but that is exactly what you are doing right now."

Her face fell to the floor with sadness. She was slipping away and R.J. knew it. The only way to bring her back was to tell her the tragic truth about his mothers' death. Nobody except for his mother knew the truth. And now he was about to tell Valarie. He only hoped that she understood.

R.J.s stomach tightened and his face went from weak to stern. Valarie had cracked his shell. What he had never before spoke about, exploded out of him like the yolk from a falling egg.

"What I never told you is that my mother had full blown Aids when she died."

Valarie's face changed from doubtful, to sympathetic, to shame. She let go of his hand and through her hands around him like she could protect him from whatever memory he was having.

"I'm sorry for that baby. But its okay, you could've told me."

R.J. was resistant to her hug and unresponsive to her words. His heart was too heavy to accept her affection. He locked both of his hands underneath her armpits and backed out of her embrace.

Valarie looked towards him. He stood about an arm's length away from her and looked down into her face with a angry truth about to come out of him.

"That's not all."

Valarie was still trying to be affectionate.

"It's okay baby."

She reached out to hug him again but he rejected it with a bit of an attitude.

"Stop Valarie! Just stop! I don't deserve your affection."

"Baby, it's not your fault. Stop being so hard on yourself."

"You don't understand… I am not being hard enough on myself."

"Baby stop."

"No Valarie you really don't understand! It's not Randy's fault that my mother died, it's my fault!"

Valarie suddenly looked confused but she continued with her effort to console him.

"No it wasn't R.J. and—"

R.J. felt a burning urge to cut her off and continue with his confession.

"It wasn't Randy's fault that she died, it was mine… not only am I the one who found her dead but I am also the one who killed her!"

Valarie's mouth dropped open. She looked thunderstruck. A nurse came in to check on the baby but stopped two steps after entering the room. She looked at the couple, it was obvious that her timing couldn't have been worse, but she had a job to do. Concerned with the baby first, she paced over to the incubator to find baby Andy fast asleep.

She turned her attention to Valarie. At first she looked like she was afraid to speak but she did anyway.

"How are you feeling?"

"I am okay, but can you please give us a few minutes?"

The nurse stuttered as if she was nervous.

"Umm… umm… sure. I-I-I will be out of here shortly. Let me just check on you and your baby's vitals and I will be out of the way."

Valarie returned her eyes to her husband.

CHAPTER 11.

The two of them were sitting on Valarie's hospital bed staring at two different spots on the floor. They seemed completely lost in their own thoughts. They hadn't said a word to each other since the nurse had come in and they paid her little attention as she moved swiftly around the room. The only speaking that was done was when Valarie answered the typical questions asked by the nurse. The couple anxiously awaited the nurse's departure from the room.

When the nurse was done with her duties, she left the room in a hurry. As if she was just as anxious to be away from them as they wished for her to be.

As soon as the door shut behind the nurse, they lifted their heads at the same time and looked into each other's face. Valarie looked at a loss for words, at the same time, like she had many questions scrambling through her head and she didn't know which one to ask first.

R.J. read her mind.

"I know that you have a lot of questions and I hope that what I'm about to tell you answers them all."

Valarie opened her mouth but R.J. stopped her from speaking.

"Please don't say anything until I'm finished. I really need you to listen. When I'm done telling you what I have to tell you, then you can ask me anything you want… and you can judge me as you see fit."

He paused to take a look at their baby, and then he looked back at his wife.

"Just know that I don't care about anybody's judgment… Because if I had to do what I did all over again, I would."

Valarie leaned back on her pillow and looked at him with listening eyes. He had her undivided attention. R.J. cleared his throat…

æææææææææææææææææææææææææææ

"Everything started to go wrong when I was in the sixth grade. I was only eleven. My grandmother and my mother had a huge fight and my grandmother threw my mother out of her house. My mother packed up what little belongings she had, along with me, and moved out on her own. For whatever reason my grandmother kept my sister with her; and my father, well by this time I barely ever saw him.

The neighborhood we moved to was rundown and drug infested. I believe that the area was all that my mother could afford.

Halfway through my sixth grade school year, my mother began to get sick. She was constantly in and out of the hospital. Sometimes she stayed for a couple of days and sometimes she stayed for a couple of weeks. She told me that she had been diagnosed with having H.I.V... She wanted me to go and to stay with my grandmother, but I refused too. I told her that I would never leave her side. She tried to force me to leave but I wouldn't go.

The apartment we moved into was closer to the hospital than my grandmother's house was so that's where I wanted to be. Even when she was in the hospital and I was supposed to be going to my grandmother's house after school, I still refused to go. I had my own key to the apartment so I would go to school and afterwards I would go to the apartment and stay by myself. Sometimes I was afraid to be alone but I dealt with it because I wanted to be as close to my mother as I possibly could.

On many of the nights I didn't have anything to eat so I would go into the corner store and steal a bag of chips or whatever else I could get away with. Then I got caught. The store owner screamed at me and threatened to call the police on me. All I could do was cry. I didn't want him to call the police because of what my mother had told me when I asked her where my daddy was at. She simply said that he had done something bad and the police had come and taken him away. I knew that if the police took me away, then I would no longer be able to see my mother.

While the store owner was shouting at me, a guy from the neighborhood named Thomas came into the store. I knew the guy's name was Thomas because I use to see him talking to my mother a lot. Thomas came to my aid by paying the store owner for the bag of chips that would have been my dinner. He told me not to steal again, and then he asked me why he hadn't been seeing my mother lately.

I told him that she was in the hospital and that I was staying in the apartment by myself and I didn't have any money for food so that's why I was stealing. From that day forward he gave me money every day and told me to always keep the door locked.

By the time summer hit, things were getting worse. My mother began staying in the hospital for longer periods of time. After each hospital visit, she came home a physically smaller and weaker person. In the blink of an eye, she went from being an out and about beautiful lady, to looking sick and she began to move around like it hurt her to simply walk. Her always high spirits had been broken and my mother had all together come to an all-time low.

When my seventh grade school year came in, her illness had taken complete control of her body. The H.I.V. had grown to full blown A.I.D.S. and she started looking like a ghost. Her smooth skin had dried up and looked like rough leather. The weight of her nice body had been stripped from her. Her shoulders were as thin as metal clothes hangers and all of the clothes that use to fit tight and make her appealing, were now hanging off of her like window curtains.

Her face was sucked in so far that it exposed the skeleton of her cheekbones and she no longer had pretty brown eyes. She had the eyes of someone who was trapped in a recurring horror. This transformation happened right in front of my face.

She use to suffer so much... Sometimes when she was in pain, she found the strength to get herself dressed and she would go outside to the store. She would always try to stop me from going with her, but she couldn't. I guess she thought that I was embarrassed by her, but I wasn't. We would go outside and all of the people that we encountered seem to always give her some type of uncomfortable look. It used to make me so upset but to me, they all were the ugly ones and my mother was the beauty.

The only person who treated my mother with dignity was the guy Thomas. She would stop and start talking to him and she would send me upstairs with whatever we had gotten from the store. A few moments later she would come upstairs behind me. That's when I noticed a pattern...

It seemed that every time she was in pain and barely able to get out of bed, she would get dressed and we would walk to the store. During each store visit she stopped and had a short conversation with Thomas. After every conversation with him, not long afterwards, she suddenly felt better. I called their conversations miracle talks. I really wondered what he was saying to her to make her feel better. She would be suddenly able to move around the house with ease.

She would cook and clean and sometimes even had enough strength left to watch T.V. with me. We'd always watch Wheel of Fortune and during the show we would battle to see who got the most puzzles correct. She won almost every round and the times that she didn't win was the times when she wanted me to win. Afterwards we would answer a few questions that were inside of the little book she had with the diamond on the cover. We had so much fun together.

One day I was on my way home from school and I saw the police shoving Thomas into the back of a cop car with his hands cuffed behind his back. I ran up the stairs and told my mother what I had seen. When I told her she literally crawled out of the bed over to the window. She stood there staring out of that window until she was too weak to stand. Then she crawled back into bed looking defeated; like she had lost her best friend. I felt her pain and right then and there I knew there would be no more miracle talks. I was right, and soon after Thomas had gotten taken away, she was back to being in and out of the hospital.

She frequented the hospital so much that it wasn't long before her insurance ran out. That left her with no way to pay her hospital bills or to fill her prescriptions to get her medication. She was sentenced to suffer with-in the four walls of that apartment. She was left to depend on me. I wasn't even a teenager and I had to take on the responsibility of taking care of her. I had to try to figure out how to take away her pain.

I did everything I could to help her but she needed so much more than the little bit of help that I was able to offer her. She was so sick and in so much pain that at times I didn't want to go to school. It didn't feel right leaving her in that apartment by herself in the condition that she was in. She couldn't do anything for herself but she still made me go to school. She told me that nothing in the world would make her happier than to see me graduate, so I never missed a day. And I made sure I received all A's.

Every morning before I left for school, even if she was asleep, I made sure I fixed her something to eat and something to drink. Then I would place it with-in her reach. More importantly, every morning before I left out, I gave her a kiss on her lips and told her that I loved her and told her that I would be back to help her as soon as I got out of school.

My mother was getting sick at a pace so rapid that it wasn't long before she weighed about eighty pounds.

Every day I rushed off to school hoping that the day would go by quicker than the day before so I could hurry home to be with my mother. I sat in class watching the clock, but the time never sped up for me.

A lot of days when I made it home I would see her lying there crying and frowning in pain while she laid in her bed in a puddle of her own waste. At times, she didn't even notice that I had come in from school. She wouldn't even be aware that I was in the same room with her. Sometimes I would clean her up then sit there with her and watch her squirm in pain until she fell asleep. Other times I cleaned her up then went into another room and cried my little heart out. I begged God to give me the power needed to take away my mother's pain. I was willing to do anything. If there was something at the ends of the earth that would take away my mother's pain, I was willing to walk there to get it. Then God answered my prayers.

One day when I came home from school, my mother's face was soaked in tears. Snot surrounded her nose and she was coughing up mucus. She would cough then let out a loud painful moan behind it. She sounded like she was being hit in the chest with a brick. I wished that there was someone who we could turn to for help. I missed Thomas so much…

While she was crying, I brought a whole roll of tissue to her bedside and used the entire roll to clean her messy face and wipe away the millions of tears that she cried. When I was done, I asked her a question; and her answer turned me into an angel sent by a demon.

"Mommy"

I said.

"How come every time you talked to Thomas it made you feel better? What was he saying to you? If you tell me, I will say the same thing to you and maybe it will make you feel better."

My question broke the heart in her eyes and the tears that I had just wiped away returned. I thought that I had said something wrong so I apologized.

"I'm sorry mommy; I didn't mean to make you cry again."

Her eyes were glassy. She tried to smile. Her voice was weak.

"It's okay R.J... you didn't say anything wrong."

With the little strength she had, she lifted her bony hand and patted the bed as a gesture for me to sit down beside her. I did as she requested but when I sat down, I must've done so too quickly because the bounce of the bed caused her to grunt with pain.

"I'm sorry mommy."

She coughed then closed her eyes and cleared her throat. She was in so much pain that I hurt for her.

"Don't worry about it baby. You didn't know that would hurt me."

She reached out and placed her skinny fingers on top of my hand. I turned my small hand over so that our palms were touching and I held her hand with as much tenderness as I could. Her hand had no warmth. Her fingers were so cold that it felt like she didn't have any blood circulating in them. I was afraid to move my fingers because I thought that even the slightest squeeze would break every bone in her hand. My mother closed her eyes in an attempt to find strength then she cleared her throat and explained what the truth really was behind her and Thomas so called 'miracle talks'.

"Randy junior."

She said.

"Thomas didn't say anything special to me to make me feel better."

She hesitated. And before she spoke again, I felt her fingers trying to move. I looked down and saw that she was trying to tighten her grip around my hand. It was clear that she was too weak. She fought with a cough but never let her eyes fall from my face.

"R.J., Thomas wasn't a good guy baby. He just had something that made me feel good."

I was confused. Thomas had given me money to eat. I really believed that he was a nice guy so I pushed the thoughts of if he was a good guy or not out of my head. I didn't care one way or the other. I just wanted to know what it was that he gave her...

"What did he give you mommy?"

"It was a bad thing baby."

"It couldn't have been bad if it made you feel good. What was it?"

She looked like she was about to confess a terrible sin.

"He gave me a drug baby; the worst drug in the world. He gave me something called heroin."

After she told me that, she closed her eyes and just laid there. I sat at her side and watched over her like I was her guardian angel until I was sure she had fallen asleep. Even in her sleep, she couldn't escape the suffering. She moaned and let out spurts of painful cries. I sat there in silence and watched and listened to her suffering for as long as I could. Then I realized what I had to do... I had to go out and find my mother some heroin...

I had no idea what heroin was but I set off on a mission to find some and locating some heroin turned out to be one of the easiest things that I ever had to do. All I had to do was open my front door. In the hallway there was a lady; a lady who always sat on the steps begging for change.

When I walked into the hallway, she was there in her usual spot at the bottom of a flight of stairs. She wasn't begging. Something was wrong with her. She was curled over with her arms folded across her stomach; her head hung towards the floor and the tangled locks of her hair needed to be washed. She held her stomach and rocked back and forth. I approached her carefully and when I got close to her I heard the sounds of her moans and grunts. A chill shot up my spine. She sounded just like my mother; like she was in just as much pain. I stopped in front of her and her body odor caused both of my hands to fly up to my face and cover my nose and mouth. It smelled like she had used the bathroom on herself. She really reminded me all too much of my mother.

I whispered at her.

"Excuse me ma'am."

She stopped rocking for a second but never stopped moaning as she lifted her head to me; but before she could get a good look at me, her head dropped back down and dangled loosely.

"Owwww!"

She sounded like someone who had had enough. Her voice was groggy.

"Leave me alone… Get away from me."

I wasn't going to leave until I had asked her what I came to ask.

"I'm sorry to bother you but can---"

Her head jumped up and she screamed.

"Get away from me!!!"

I flinched in fear, but stood my ground. She stared at me with hollow eyes. I was scared but refused to run away. I was willing to face anything if I thought it would help my mother. The lady's head dropped back down into her lap. I built up the courage to speak again.

"I just want to ask you one question."

She ignored me and continued to groan, but what I said next caught me her attention.

"*I just want to ask you if you know where I could get some heroin from.*"

She immediately stopped both rocking and moaning. Slowly her head rose up until her eyes were resting on my face. The hollowness that I saw before was gone. Some kind of hope had taken its place.

She leaped up and reached for me but she didn't have enough strength to stand so she ended up down in a kneeling position directly in front of me. Her hands grabbed me at the sides of both of my arms. I was caught by surprise. She looked psychotic and I had to stop myself from pulling away and running from her.

Her lips were so dry and cracked to a point where it looked like you could almost see blood.

She began to beg.

"*Do you have some heroin? I'll do anything you want me to do! Please! Just give me a little bit so that I won't be sick!*"

"*I don't have any but I'm trying to get some for my mother. She is sick too and I am trying to help her.*"

"*Do you have any money?*"

I knew that my mother kept her money inside of the little black book with the diamond on the cover. The book next to the T.V. and she always took some money out of it before she went to the store to talk to Thomas.

"*How much do you need?*"

She looked at me like she wanted to lie but I think she told me the truth.

"Give me twenty dollars and I will get enough to make me and your mother feel better."

I got excited.

"Wait right here! I will be right back!"

I turned around and rushed back into the apartment. The book was sitting next to the T.V. as it always was. My heart skipped a beat. I didn't know for sure if there was money inside of it or not, and even if it was, I didn't know if it was at least twenty dollars. I picked the book up and held my breath, and then I opened the book.

I was relieved to see a total of about ninety dollars. I grabbed a twenty dollar bill and slammed the book shut and put it back where it belonged. I turned to leave and my eyes landed on my mother's helpless body. She was in a deep and painful sleep. Her head tossed to one side and then to the other. Her face was wet. She was trapped in a cold sweat. I walked over to her bedside.

I knew that she couldn't hear me but I spoke anyway.

"I'm not stealing from you mommy. I would never do that, okay."

I stood there for a few seconds like I was waiting for her to respond. Gently I leaned in and kissed her on the side of her sweaty face.

"I'll be right back... I'm going to get you some help."

In a hurry, I ran back to the door hoping that the lady was still where I left her. I walked back out into the hallway and was happy to see that she hadn't moved. She was still on bended knees and still had that cry for help look in her eyes.

I walked up to her with my hand stretched out holding the money. She bounced up to her feet like she was no longer in pain and snatched the money from my hand.

"I will be right back."

She took off speed walking before I could say a word. I was left standing there alone with the terrible stench of her body odor. A puddle of urine was on the step where she was sitting. I was happy that I could help her, and even happier that i was about to help my mother. I stood in the hallway by myself and prayed for her to come back. And she did.

She was back with-in fifteen minutes.

When she returned she handed me a tiny envelope. It looked like it contained some type of beige powdery looking substance. I shoved the tiny looking envelope into my pocket then me and the lady agreed to meet in the hallway at the same time every day so that she could get me some heroin for my mother. I left the hallway and went and sat patiently at my mothers bedside.

I sat there helplessly watching her fight off whatever demons she had to face while she slept. I fought off the urge to wake her. occasionally I took the small envelope out of my pocket and stared at it. I would look at my mother in all of her pain then I would back at the envelope and wondered what type of magical powers the beige powder had to be able to take away so much pain.

Two hours later, my mother opened her eyes.

When she saw me sitting there watching over her, she cracked a faint smile that caused her face to twist in pain. Her expression tore at my heart and I wasn't about to sit there like I didn't have the only thing that could take away the pain. I had to tell her the good news about me finding her some heroin.

I jumped to my feet. Her helpless face watched me closely. I pulled the tiny envelope out from my pocket and held it out to her. I was over excited. I had finally found a way to help my mother.

"Look mommy! Look what i have for you!"

She looked at me like I was crazy.

Her face frowned up in horror when she saw what it was that I was holding in my hand. Tears filled her eyes and poured relentlessly. She started to cough uncontrollably. I dropped the small envelope on the floor and reached to aid her. All of a sudden, she had a new found strength. She raised her arm and shoved me away from her. It frightened me and I was puzzled.

Without my assistance, she was able to get her coughing under control, then she pointed to the floor at the envelope. I knew that she wanted me to pick it up but I was afraid. Not only that, but I didn't want to frighten her again. She pointed harder and I figured that it was okay to pick the heroin up. I reached down and scooped it into my hand then I stuck my hand out to give it to her. She reached out but didn't take it. Instead her fragile fingers took hold of my entire hand and she pulled me until I was sitting down on her bed beside her. She looked deeper into my eyes then she ever had.

"Where did you get this from?"

She never let go of my hand; never stopped looking in my eyes; and sat quietly as I told her about the lady in the hallway and the arrangement that we had made.

When I was done she said,

"Although I will be dead and gone when you are old enough to understand what's happening right now, I hope that you will still find it in your heart to forgive me."

She took the envelope out of my hand and asked me to excuse myself from the room. Twenty minutes later she called out my name.

I returned to her room and it made my heart happy to see that she was sitting upright with her legs hanging off of her bed. She smiled at me with guilty eyes. I went and sat beside her. My mother had enough strength to wrap her arms around me and to pull me into her chest. She kissed me on the top of my head. That night we watched wheel of fortune and she got every puzzle right. After that, she picked up the little book with *the diamond on the cover and we had fun answering some of the questions.*

For the next few days everything was okay. The rest of the world didn't matter. My mother was strong enough to move around. We didn't need anyone. I had her and she had me. She was still weaker than the average person but she was functional and we had some nice times together.

Then it happened...

CHAPTER 12.

It was four days after I made the agreement with the lady in the hallway, at somewhere around five a.m.

I was lying beside my mother tossing and turning, dozing in and out of my sleep. I couldn't rest comfortably because the day before my father had stopped by. I was having thoughts of how I use to love him so much, but had grown to hate him even more. Something mysteriously snatched me out of my thoughts.

I popped up and looked over to my mother, (before I dozed off she had asked me to see my notebook so that she could write in it). She was still awake, but she was no longer writing. My notebook sat next to her and she was having a really strange coughing attack. I was used to hearing her cough uncontrollably with phlegm rattling roughly in her throat. This time it wasn't like that; this time she was wheezing and coughing softly. Her wind was weak.

I knew something was wrong. I jumped up and turned on the light. The sudden brightness made her blink. When her vision adjusted, we met eyes and stared at each other for a long second... Then, without warning, a monstrous cough attack like never before overtook her. The rattle in her throat was thick. The tears in her eyes were many.

I panicked...

"Mommy are you okay? Mommy! Mommy!"

She continued to cough.

"Do you need some water mommy?"

She was able to shake her head up and down. I jumped up and rushed to the kitchen and made her a glass of water. When I returned, she was sitting up holding her stomach and groaning. Her face was covered in sweat and she winced in pain. I could tell that she needed some heroin.

I sat the glass of water down and rushed over to the little book with the diamond on it to get some money. I snatched the book open and grabbed the money out of it. I looked at her suffering and all I wanted to do was help.

"I'll be right back mommy okay!"

She looked like she wanted to say something but couldn't. I wanted to know what she was trying to say, but I had to hurry to get her some heroin so I just turned around and shot out the door. When I got into the hallway I looked around frantically for the lady that I had made the arrangement with. I didn't see her. I ran up the stairs to the top floor but she was nowhere to be found. I turned around and shot back down the stairs out of the building into the street. There wasn't a person in sight. The neighborhood looked like a ghost town. I looked in every direction but didn't know which way to go. My feet just started to move and I ended up heading towards the store that I had gotten caught stealing in.

I had never run so fast or pushed myself so hard. As I rounded the corner, I crashed into someone and my small body went flying to the ground. It felt like I had run into a brick wall. I think the wind was knocked out of me but I recovered quickly. I was back on my feet in a split second. I didn't even acknowledge the person that I had run into, I just tried to take off running again but the person grabbed me by my arm. I tried to tug away but they wouldn't let me go. I was about to yell at the person for them to let me go but when I looked up I was too shocked to say anything. The person that I had run into was the only person in the world that could help me and my mother. My lady friend from the hallway.

She was saying something to me but I screamed over her words.

"My mother!!! She needs help!!! She's never been this sick and she really needs some heroin!!!"

I reached into my pocket and pulled out the money and tried to shove it into her hand but she didn't take it.

"Please!!! Please!!! Please take the money and go and get her some heroin!!! Please!!!"

The lady looked away from me down at her purse and stuck her hand into her bag.

"Just calm down... you don't have to give me any money. I have some heroin and you can give her some of mines."

I couldn't believe my ears. Before she could get her hand all the way out of the purse I dropped the money and reached out and snatched the heroin from her hand. I turned around and took off running back towards my building.

I was moving faster than I was before I had the heroin. I reached the building and took the steps two at a time. When I reached the floor that our apartment was on I charged for our house and almost knocked the door down trying to get inside. My mother was still coughing and groaning. I rushed over to her and forced the heroin into her hand.

"Hurry up mommy!!! Hurry up so that you could feel better!!!"

I turned around and was about to excuse myself so that she could do what she needed to do but I felt her skinny hand grab my wrist. I turned around and looked up at my mother. She looked so sad. Like she knew something but didn't want to tell me. I felt her hand trying to squeeze my arm.

"I love you R. J."

"I love you too mommy."

"Give me a kiss."

I kissed her on her dry lips then backed away from her.

"Hurry up mommy! Hurry up and do what you do with the heroin so that you could feel better!"

She smiled at me and I went into the other room. I stood directly behind the door and waited for my mother to call my name like she did ever time after she got the heroin. I waited and I waited and I waited. She never called me. After about thirty minutes I decided to open her room door. My mother was lying on her back on her bed with her eyes wide open.

I stood in the doorway already knowing that she was gone but I didn't want to believe it. I took one step towards her and whispered her name.

"Mommy..."

She didn't respond. I took another step and my voice rose a little.

"Mommy..."

Her eyes didn't even move. By now I was at her bedside and all I could do was scream.

"Mommy!!!"

She was gone. My mother was gone. My head dropped and right there on the floor was the tiny envelope. It no longer had the heroin in it. She had used the heroin that I had given her. I had given my mother the heroin to help her but instead it killed her.

A.R. Dash   My Mother's Diary

I had killed my mother…

CHAPTER 13.

When R.J. finished telling his story, Valarie was sitting there with tears falling from her eyes.

She wrapped her arms around him.

"You didn't kill her R.J., you were only trying to help."

R.J. backed away and looked at her.

"I never meant to hurt you Valarie… I've been holding this secret in for years and it's been eating me alive. I always felt as though it was the heroin that I gave her that killed her. Then, when Randy showed up with the diary, I felt like I finally had someone to point the finger at besides myself. I never wanted you to know about any of this but now you do. You know everything. Please forgive me; I'm still the man that you fell in love with, just minus the dark secret."

They hugged each other and R.J. knew that he had done the right thing by telling her what he had never told anyone else. The hospital room door opened and to both of their surprise, R.J.s sister Rachel was walking into the room. In one hand she carried some type of gift for the new baby and in the other hand she had a notebook. The couple let go of each other and Valarie got up to welcome R. J.s sister

"Hello Rachel."

"Hello sister-in-law. I've been trying to reach you guys forever. Then my father stopped by and told me what happened."

R.J. and his sister met eyes.

"Anyway… I came by to see my new nephew."

Rachel walked over to the incubator.

"Awww! He's adorable. He looks just like me."

All three of them started laughing.

"What's his name?"

Valarie told her how the name was a mixture of their mother and R.J.s names. Rachel thought it was a beautiful gesture then she turned to her brother and reminded him of something that he had truly forgotten about because of all that was going on.

"If you could have made her keep that baby in her stomach for two more days, he would've been born on the same day that mommy died."

R.J. thought about it. His sister was right. The fifteenth anniversary of his mother's death was only two days away.

R.J. felt a wave of guilt. He had always been too ashamed to visit her gravesite.

Rachel must've sensed his unease because she changed the subject.

"But anyway R.J., I've had this in my possession for a long time."

R.J. felt a sense of panic. Those were the same exact words that Randy said before he told R.J. about his mother's diary. Valarie and R.J. looked at each other. Rachel held the notebook out to him.

"I think you need to read this."

R.J. politely pushed the book away.

"Noooo thank you. I think I had enough to read."

"Please R.J… After what Randy told me, this might make you feel better."

R.J looked down and couldn't believe his eyes. Rachel was holding his old notebook. The same notebook that his mother had been writing in that morning before she died. He reached out and took it into his hands then he stood there and read what his mother's final thoughts were before she passed away.

∞∞∞∞∞∞∞∞∞∞∞∞∞∞∞∞∞∞∞∞∞∞∞∞∞∞∞∞∞∞∞∞

Today is the day that I'm going to die. I know it. I can feel it. I've never been this weak. It's so cold. Everything hurts. I barely have enough strength to hold this pen. I don't know how much longer I can write. I'm finally scared. I have so much to say but don't think I have the time I need to say it all. So with my last breath, I send you these words.

Dear Lord, I would like to thank you for the gift of allowing me to spend my last days with my son R.J... There's no paradise that awaits me that could compare to that. Thank you. But Lord, he's not going to take my death easy, that's why I gave Randy my diary and asked him to never show it to R.J... I wouldn't want my son to know about all of those things that went on between me and Randy. There's no telling what he will do.

And Lord, Please know that I'm bringing no grudges with me. I even forgave Randy. Please know that---

∞∞∞∞∞∞∞∞∞∞∞∞∞∞∞∞∞∞∞∞∞∞∞∞∞∞∞∞∞∞∞∞∞∞∞∞∞∞

That is all that was written in R.J.s notebook. The incomplete sentence must've been when she started to have the cough attack that brought R.J. out of his thoughts. R.J. stood there amazed... He couldn't believe that the diary hadn't been stolen, but in fact, his mother had given the diary to Randy to protect R.J.s feelings.

R.J. closed the book...

THE END...

→

→

Epilogue

The graveyard was just as gloomy as the dark sky…

Today marked the fifteenth anniversary of R.J.s mother death, but it was only the first time that he had been to visit her gravesite.

Gray clouds covered the sky like a thick blanket. R.J. had just stepped out of the car. The light drizzle of rain felt like soft kisses from heaven falling upon his head. Neither butterflies nor nervousness could explain the feelings that were flying through his body. He turned his head and his lovely wife Valarie came into his view. She was supportive as well as beautiful.

Anxiety showed on his face and she walked up to him and gently placed her hand on the outside of his.

"It's going to be okay R.J."

Her words were soothing and re-assuring. Looking into her face, he saw that her pretty brown eyes were full of concern. His eyes left her face and landed on the ground. This was going to be harder than he thought. He took a deep breath in an attempt to suck the courage he needed into his body out of the thin air. Then he let out a hard sigh.

Valarie put a finger underneath his chin and lifted his head until their eyes met. She didn't say a word and she didn't have too. R.J. knew exactly what it was that she was thinking. 'He had to go through with this'.

Since his mother's death, he had been so ashamed of himself for giving his mother heroin, he allowed any and everything to come between him and this place. This very place of sanctuary; this place of holiness; this place where the woman who had given him life, was to rest for the remainder of all eternity.

He stood there momentarily frozen with fear. He tried to swallow but his mouth was to dry; tried to move his legs but his feet were too heavy. Something seemed to have a hold on him. He squeezed his wife's hand for strength and suddenly was able to move. Without letting go of Valarie's hand, he began to lead the way to his mother's grave site.

They had to walk on grass that covered people's graves. The grass was wet and unusually soft and gave R.J. unwanted thoughts but he continued to move forward. On both sides of them, there were rows and rows of gray tombstones. It didn't feel right to R.J. to be walking over peoples place of rest so as they walked, he begin to read the names on the tombs that they passed. Silently, he apologized for him and his wife's unintentional disrespect.

R.J. lifted his head and looked across the graveyard. It was a horizon of death. Thousands of stone gray tombs neatly aligned every inch of the cemetery. For a reason that R.J. was unaware of, he found himself wondering what it was like to be dead. Fear of the unknown quickly invaded him, but before he could react to it, it escaped him. He looked over to Valarie. She appeared to be handling the journey better than he was. She squeezed his hand to let him know that she was there for him. His mother' grave was just ahead…

Unconsciously he slowed his pace. Suddenly Valarie let go of his hand. He was startled and he looked over to her.

"This is something that you have to do on your own R.J., but I am right here if you need me."

R.J. wanted to protest but he couldn't find the words. She was right and he took the last few steps alone. He stopped directly in front of his mother's grave. He couldn't believe that he was standing in front of the rock in the ground that was set to hold his mother's legacy. He read the words that were carved into the stone.

'In loving memory or Shirley Ann Madison'

His heart pounded and then sank. A lonely tear raced down his face and dived off of his chin into the grass that covered his mother's casket.

A blinding streak of lightning cracked the sky and an ear shattering clap of thunder shook the earth. R.J. jerked his head up to make sure that his wife was okay. She was, but what R.J. saw as he looked in her direction caused him to jerk in surprise.

Over Valarie's shoulder, and in the distance, he saw his father Randy approaching. R.J. took a deep breath and another blinding streak of lightening shot across the sky…

To see what's next to come from your new favorite author

<u>A.R. DASH</u>

Turn the page;

Hold your breath;

And be prepared for anything…

ALSO

IF YOU SHARE WITH SOMEONE A BOND THAT IS EVEN HALF AS CLOSE AS THE BOND THAT R.J. SHARED WITH HIS MOTHER, YOU CAN

PURCHASE YOUR VERY OWN DIGITAL VERSION OF THE CRYSTAL DIAMOND DIARY IN THE SAME WAY THAT YOU PURCHASED THIS BOOK.

THE DIGITAL VERSION DOES NOT CONTAIN THE SECTIONS IN WHICH YOU CAN PHYSICALLY WRITE IN BUT IT DOES CONTAIN ALL OF THE INTERESTING QUESTIONS THAT R.J. SHARED WITH HIS MOTHER.

BUT BE CAREFUL; BECAUSE THE CRYSTAL DIAMOND DIARY IS KNOWN

TO CREATE BONDS THAT LAST FOREVER....

X&O

BY

A.R. DASH

Prologue

Kevin jumped up out of his sleep. The thumping in his head felt like a sledge hammer striking his temples again and again. The night before he'd had too much to drink. Now he was suffering a major hangover.

"Bang!- Bang!"

Kevin wanted to scream. He grabbed the sides of his temples and squeezed his eyes closed tightly but there was no way for him to shake his headache. The pounding got louder.

"Bang!- Bang!"

The sound was so loud that it made his body jerk. Kevin opened his eyes and looked at the front door.

"Bang!- Bang!- Bang!! Bang!! Bang!!"

Somebody was trying to knock his front door off of its hinges.

Kevin snatched the covers from around him and flung them to the floor in frustration. Then he lunged up off of his twin size bed mad at the world. He looked at his digital wrist watch. It was 6:31 a.m.

Who in their right mind could be foolish enough to be at his door this time of the morning acting like they didn't have any good sense. The steps that Kevin took towards the door probably shook the chandelier on the ceiling of the neighbors beneath him. The door was unlocked.

Whomever it was on the other side was wasting their time with all of the commotion. If they wanted to get to Kevin so badly, all they had to do was turn the knob and walk in; or anyone else for that matter could have just walked in. The carelessness was due to Kevin's drinking problem. He had to get a grip on himself and on his drinking. The person on the other side of the door continued with their assault on the helpless door.

"Bang! Bang! Bang!"

Kevin had had enough. He was about arms reach away from the door and didn't bother to ask who it was. He didn't ask, nor did he care who it was. It could've been the president; whoever it was on the other side of that door was about to get a nasty piece of Kevin's mind.

Kevin grabbed the door knob and yanked the door open. Danny stood there clutching a silver handgun down at his side. Kevin froze but he wasn't afraid. The nasty words that he wanted to say were still tempting to leave his mouth, but he stood quiet. Danny was Kevin's ex-wife new boyfriend.

Danny slowly raised the bun until it was pointing at Kevin's face. Kevin took a deep breath but didn't blink, neither did Danny. Danny looked calm but dangerous. His jawbone was tight with clenched teeth. Murder rested in the dark pupils of his slanted eyes.

"Kevin, if my son dies, so do you..."

Kevin didn't respond. For a split second, Kevin entertained the thought of trying to snatch the gun out of Danny's hand. The thought came and went because if he did try to snatch the gun but wasn't successful, than more likely than not, it would increase the chances of Danny shooting him.

The muscles in Danny's jaw flexed in anger. And with the gun just inches away from Kevin's head, Danny slowly began to back away. His words were just as calm and dangerous as the look on his face.

"Today is Wednesday Kevin...the doctors only gave him seven more days to live...that means that you have about six days to save my little boy."

Danny got quiet for a second, like he wanted to make sure that his next words were heard clearly and sunk into Kevin's head.

"If you don't help my little boy and you let him die, not even the good Lord himself is going to be able to save you from me."

The words were haunting.

"Do the right thing Kevin."

Danny turned and walked away. Kevin watched him until he was no longer in sight. For many minutes after Danny was gone, Kevin stood in his door way having a vision.

In the vision, Kevin was the one holding Danny at gunpoint, but he gave no threats or warnings. Instead, while Kevin held the gun to Danny's face, he thought about how Danny had destroyed his family and taken everything of value that Kevin had away from him.

Kevin was the furthest thing in the world from a killer, but in this vision, he pointed the gun at Danny and without a second thought, he repeatedly squeezed the trigger until there wasn't a bullet left in the gun. Then he took back all that Danny had taken from him.

Kevin came back to reality and slammed his front door. It was even seven a.m. and Kevin found himself pouring a drink. Then he laughed out loud at Danny's threat. There was no way that he was going to help the man's child. Especially since the mother of the child was also the mother of his sixteen year old twin boys.

www.ingramcontent.com/pod-product-compliance
Lightning Source LLC
LaVergne TN
LVHW051554070426
835507LV00021B/2572